IMAGES OF ASIA

Dance in Cambodia

Titles in the series

Dance in Cambodia

TONI SAMANTHA PHIM
AND
ASHLEY THOMPSON

OXFORD
UNIVERSITY PRESS

OXFORD
UNIVERSITY PRESS

4 Jalan Pemaju U1/15, Seksyen U1, 40150 Shah Alam,
Selangor Darul Ehsan, Malaysia

Oxford University Press is a department of the University of Oxford.
It furthers the University's objective of excellence in research, scholarship,
and education by publishing worldwide in

Oxford New York

Athens Auckland Bangkok Bogotá Buenos Aires Calcutta
Cape Town Chennai Dar es Salaam Delhi Florence Hong Kong Istanbul
Karachi Kuala Lumpur Madrid Melbourne Mexico City Mumbai
Nairobi Paris São Paulo Singapore Taipei Tokyo Toronto Warsaw

with associated companies in Berlin Ibadan

Oxford is a registered trade mark of Oxford University Press
in the UK and in certain other countries

Published in the United States
by Oxford University Press, New York

British Library Cataloguing in Publication Data

Data Available

Library of Congress Cataloging-in-Publication Data
Phim, Toni Samantha.
Dance in Cambodia/Toni Samantha Phim and Ashley Thompson.
p.   cm.—(Images of Asia)
Includes bibliographical references (p.) and index.
ISBN 983 56 0059 7
1. Dance—Cambodia.   2. Cambodia—Social life and customs.
I. Thompson, Ashley.   II. Title.   III. Series
GV1703.C3P55
1999
792. 8' 09596—dc21

Typeset by Indah Photosetting Centre Sdn. Bhd., Malaysia
Printed by Printmate Sdn. Bhd., Kuala Lumpur
Published by Penerbit Fajar Bakti Sdn. Bhd. (008974-T)
under licence from Oxford University Press

Acknowledgements

WE would like to express our thanks to the following people and institutions whose assistance and support have made this book possible: Ang Chouléan, Eileen Blumenthal, Carol Bracy, Patricia Bulitt, Chheng Phon, Véronique Decrop, Dale Delsing, Marianne Gerschel, Hang Chan Sophea, Hang Si Doeun, Hang Soth, Mao Keng, Kathleen McClintock, Meas Saran, Mills College Department of Dance, Princess Norodom Buppha Devi, Suppya Nut, Phan Phuong, Phim Mala, Thavro Phim, Pi Bunnin, Pich Tum Kravel, Eric Prenowitz, Proeung Chhieng, Phanh Ratsamy, Sek Sophea, Alan Shapiro, Lynn Shapiro, Peg Connor Shapiro, Anne Sheeran, Maryanne Teng, Chinary Ung, Judy Van Zile, Jean Weishan, Yith Sarin. We also want to acknowledge our deep gratitude to the many other artists in Cambodia who have shared their expertise with us.

February 1999   TONI SAMANTHA PHIM
                                                   ASHLEY THOMPSON

Contents

A Note on Music

THE rich and varied musical traditions of Cambodia include a number of ensembles with distinct repertoires. Each orchestra, whether playing for weddings, funerals, boxing matches, exorcism ceremonies, folk songs and dances, Buddhist temple rituals or parties and nightclubs, possesses particular sound properties and unique instrumentation.

Both seen and heard, traditional orchestras are integral to any dance event. As the drawings included here demonstrate, the instruments are works of art in themselves. Sculpted or inlaid decor accentuates or simply adorns their elegant forms. Instruments are fabricated by hand in both village and urban settings (Colour Plate 1).

The performance genres introduced in this book are, for the most part, accompanied by one of two musical ensembles: *pin peat* or *mohori*.

The *pin peat* (ពិណពាទ្យ) is a predominantly percussion orchestra which plays with shadow theatre, court dance, all-male dance–drama, and temple ceremonies. Such an ensemble generally consists of the following instruments:

Sralai (ស្រឡៃ): quadruple-reed hard wood or ivory instrument, akin to an oboe. An ensemble may employ both a small and a larger, lower-pitched *sralai*, or just a large one. (Plate 1).

Roneat ek (រនាតឯក): high-pitched xylophone with twenty-one wooden or bamboo keys (Plate 2).

Roneat thung (រនាតធុង): low-pitched xylophone with sixteen wooden or bamboo keys (Plate 3).

Roneat dek (រនាតដែក): xylophone with twenty-one steel keys (Plate 4).

Kong [vong] thom (គង់វង់ធំ): low-pitched circle of sixteen knobbed gongs set within a large rattan frame (Plate 5).

Kong [vong] touc (គង់វង់តូច): similar to *kong thom*, but with smaller gongs and frame, and a higher pitch; there may be sixteen or more gongs in the frame (Plate 6).

Sampho (សំភោរ): double-headed barrel drum mounted horizontally on a stand; heads covered with calf skin; played with the hands (Plate 7).

Skor thom (ស្គរធំ): large pair of barrel drums held in tilted position on stands; heads covered with cow skin; sounded with mallets (Plate 8).

Chheung (ឈឹង): small handheld brass cymbals (Plate 9).

The *mohori* (មហោរី) orchestra, combining strings with wind and percussion instruments, plays folk or entertainment music. It accompanies, among other things, lullabies, love songs, and some folk dances. The instruments usually found in this ensemble are:

Roneat ek (see *pin peat* description and Plate 2).

Roneat thung (see *pin peat* description and Plate 3).

Chheung (see *pin peat* description and Plate 9).

Khloy (ខ្លុយ): bamboo flute (Plate 10).

Tro chhe (ទ្រចេ): high-pitched, two-stringed fiddle with cylindrical resonating box made from wood, ivory, or buffalo horn; nowadays only sometimes included in *mohori* ensembles (Plate 11).

Tro sau (ទ្រសោ): two-stringed fiddle with cylindrical resonating box made from wood, bamboo, ivory, or buffalo horn and covered with snake skin (Plate 12).

Tro ou (ទ្រអ៊ូ): two-stringed fiddle with resonating box made from a coconut shell (Plate 13).

Krapeu (ក្រពើ) or *takhe* (តាខេ ឬ ត:ខេ): wooden, three-stringed plucked zither; the shape of the instrument resembles that of a crocodile [*krapeu* in Khmer, *takhe* in Thai] (Plate 14).

Khim (ឃឹម): hammered dulcimer (Plate 15).

Thaun rumanea (ថោនរុមនា): pair of drums; one goblet drum made from clay or wood with calf or snake skin head and one shallow frame drum; may replace *skor areak* (Plate 16).

Skor areak (ស្គរអារក្ស): goblet drum made from wood or clay; head covered with snake skin; may replace *thaun rumanea* (Plate 17).

Other instruments mentioned in the text:

Pey bobos or *pey* or (ប៉ីបុបុស ឬ ប៉ី): bamboo flute with double reed.
Ploy (ប្លយ): mouth organ fashioned from a gourd with bamboo pipes.

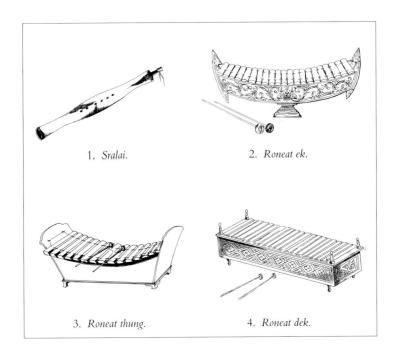

1. *Sralai.* 2. *Roneat ek.*

3. *Roneat thung.* 4. *Roneat dek.*

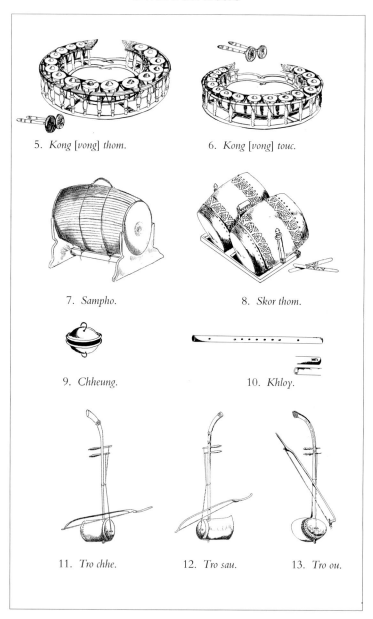

5. *Kong [vong] thom.*

6. *Kong [vong] touc.*

7. *Sampho.*

8. *Skor thom.*

9. *Chheung.*

10. *Khloy.*

11. *Tro chhe.*

12. *Tro sau.*

13. *Tro ou.*

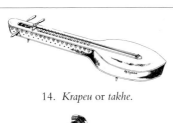

14. *Krapeu* or *takhe*.

15. *Khim.*

16. *Thaun rumanea.*

17. *Skor areak.*

(Plates 2, 5, and 6 by Y Lida; all others by Meas Saran.)

1
Introduction

Honor Self-Created Kambu whose glory (like a star) rose at the horizon, and whose superior descendance, having obtained the conjunction of the Solar and the Lunar Races, disperses ignorance […] and is perfectly complete, accomplished in all the arts.

I implore Mera, the most glorious of celestial women, whom Shiva, guru of the Three Worlds […] gave from on high as queen to this wise man.

(Inscription of Baksei Chamkrong, 10th century)[1]

THIS invocation of the mythical founders of Cambodia is part of a long Sanskrit poem that was inscribed on a stone temple doorway at Angkor in the tenth century AD. Attributing the origins of the Khmer people to the union of Kambu, a wise man, with Mera, 'most glorious of celestial women', the stanzas provide insight into the way ancient Cambodians may have seen themselves. Kambu is a man with no past, 'self-created', who none the less embodies the unification of the solar and lunar lines, a fiction undoubtedly invented to explain an early name of the country: Kambuja (pronounced *Kampuchea*), 'born of *Kambu*'. With time, this term was transformed phonetically, and gave rise to the English word Cambodia. The origins of the Khmer line are not, however, attributed solely to this miraculous man. The inscription also speaks of Mera, given as if in marriage to Kambu by Shiva, the Hindu god. Like Kambu, Mera is unknown in the Indian pantheon of religious and epic figures. And her name may likewise have been invented by the inscription's authors to explain another word for their country and people. Combining *k* from Kambu, with *mer* from Mera, the word Khmer can be seen as a product of this divine union.[2]

Progenitor of the Khmer people, Mera is one of the celestial

women commonly known in Cambodia as *apsaras*. These divinities have long been conceived by Cambodians as the model not only of femininity, but more specifically of dance. Thus, the first Cambodian woman, mother of the people, was a dancer. This tenth-century myth is now taught in Cambodian schools, and the *apsaras* are still strongly associated with the foundation of Khmer cultural and indeed national identity. The heavenly grace of these women in movement was one of the most popular themes in Angkorian art (Plate 18). The Angkorian Empire, which was centred in what is now the province of Siem Reap and stretched across much of mainland South-East Asia from the ninth to the fifteenth centuries, remains the principal source of inspiration for cultural expression in Cambodia today. The place of the *apsaras* in the collective consciousness did more than simply survive the turbulent centuries following the fall of the Empire. *Apsaras* are omnipresent in Cambodia today, carved in wood, cast in cement or metal, painted on canvas, portrayed on billboards, and displayed on storefronts. After the temple of Angkor Vat, the image of these celestial dancers is perhaps the most common icon in the country. Contemporary dancers of the classical tradition are explicitly compared with *apsaras*, breathing life into their traditional postures and gestures. They are seen as precious repositories of Cambodia's past and as such, the guarantors of her future. Dance is commonly perceived as innate to the Khmer people, and essential to the perpetuation of Cambodia as a cultural and political entity.

From a historical point of view, dance has always played a primordial role in Khmer culture. Ancient iconographic representations

18. Late twelfth–early thirteenth-century sandstone frieze of *apsara* dancers from the Bayon Temple, Angkor. This piece once formed the lower register of a temple pediment. (Courtesy of the Musée Guimet, Paris)

of dance demonstrate the wide diversity of meaning the art once had. Visions of cosmic creation can be seen in stone reliefs and sculptures of Brahmanic gods and goddesses dancing in an originary act. The study of stone inscriptions shows that the figure of Shiva as the Lord of Dance was familiar to the ancient Khmer (Plate 19). One remarkable Tantric representation of the victory of good over

19. This tenth-century sandstone statue of a female divinity, possibly in a dance pose, was found at the Koh Ker Temple complex next to the remnants of a colossal statue thought to have represented Shiva dancing. She is most likely the god's consort. (Courtesy of the Musée Guimet, Paris)

evil known in Angkorian times is a dancing sixteen-armed, eight-headed divinity (Plate 20). Translating mythic and religious epics into spatial representation, certain figures or scenes sculpted in the round or in relief present compositions and movements strikingly similar to some of those found in Khmer dance today. Bearing witness to a thematic and graphic continuum across the Khmer arts, such sculptures can be seen as precursors to or perhaps even early documentation of dramatic dance performance (Plate 21). In one form or another—carved in niches, on lintels, pediments or walls—dancing figures animated virtually every temple built by the ancient Khmer.

While Cambodia's Sanskrit inscriptions speak in poetic terms of divine beings, inscriptions composed in the Khmer vernacular tell of real dancers associated with temples and the court. Written in AD 611, the earliest dated Khmer language inscription provides a typical example, listing dancers and musicians 'donated' to serve the gods of a particular temple, much like material offerings.[3] Many gods revered in ancient Cambodia are recognizable Indian divinities; others would seem to be indigenous spirits. In the same inscription, for example, dancers and musicians are even offered to a tree god. This may well be testimony to the ancient roots of a practice widespread in Cambodia today. Music and dance are frequently offered not only to the central Buddha image of a temple, but also to the *neak ta* (local or ancestral spirits) or other guardian spirits worshipped in villages and in minor sanctuaries on Buddhist temple grounds. Performance in and of itself is an offering to the gods. Dance troupes and orchestras are associated not only with the royal court but also with local temples and villages across the country. The art of dance is familiar and important to people from all walks of life and is intimately linked to their aspirations toward the supernatural or the divine.

Formally dominated by Theravada Buddhism, modern Khmer religious culture is the result of a rich and diverse history. An elaborate system of animist beliefs undoubtedly existed prior to the arrival of Indian cultural forms some 2,000 years ago. These beliefs have proved remarkably adaptable and continue to coexist with Theravada Buddhism today. Brahmanism, and to a lesser degree

20. Twelfth-century bronze statuette of the Tantric Hevajra.
Typical representations of Indian divinities with multiple arms
and heads take on additional meaning with this kind of dancing
figurine in which the multiple limbs seem to have captured
movement, something like a strobe photograph. (Courtesy of
the Museum für Indische Kunst, Berlin)

21. Tenth-century sandstone bas-relief at the Banteay Srei
Temple, Angkor. This monkey combat scene from the
Ramayana bears a resemblance to dramatic dance sequences
from the epic tale as they are enacted today. (Courtesy of
Missions Etrangères, Paris)

Mahayana Buddhism, dominated official religious practices from at least the sixth through the thirteenth centuries. Though they no longer serve as dominant religious systems, their forceful heritage is everywhere present for the Khmer people: in the language, in the art, and in the very landscape of Cambodia, which is dotted with Brahmanic and Mahayanic monuments. Around the fourteenth century, Theravada Buddhism became Cambodia's official faith. These cultural layers cannot be extricated one from the other in any given Khmer art form, each of which demonstrates a formidable capacity for synthesis of diverse traditions.

The fate of the Indian *Ramayana* in Cambodia is one particularly pertinent example of Khmer syncretic creation. An epic tale dedicated to the Brahmanic god Vishnu in his princely avatar Rama, the Indian *Ramayana* inspired diverse artistic production in ancient Cambodia. Allusions to the story are abundant in Cambodia's Sanskrit epigraphy. Inscriptions even mention recitations of manuscript texts, which could have been associated with dramatic performance. Stone reliefs depict scenes from the epic story (Colour Plate 2). Statues of the poem's heroes, Rama, his wife Sita, and brother Laksmana, were even worshipped in temple sanctuaries. Through artistic creation, the history of Khmer kings was assimilated with that of Rama. The *Ramayana* epic, which has multiple incarnations in India itself, took on still new forms in the Khmer mould.

One of the earliest known literary works to have been composed in the Khmer language is in fact the Khmer version of the Indian *Ramayana*, the *Reamker*. Though Khmer had long been used to record practical information, no traces remain of true literary composition in the Khmer language itself in Angkorian times. It would seem to have taken the arrival of Theravada Buddhism in the thirteenth and fourteenth centuries, with the concomitant abandonment of Sanskrit as the tool of literary composition, for Khmer literature to blossom in this way. Through such monumental changes, however, Indian culture, and particularly the *Ramayana*, remained a primary source of literary and artistic inspiration. Dated to the sixteenth or seventeenth centuries, the *Reamker* is not a direct translation of any original Indian text. The general storyline

is conserved, as are the majority of episodes common to the many adaptations of the *Ramayana* throughout Asia. Yet the Khmer text, still taught in Cambodian schools today, contains numerous episodes and innovations unique to Cambodian and other South-East Asian cultures. Such variations on the Indian model can in fact be traced to Cambodia's ancient inscriptions and reliefs. Infused also with Theravadin Buddhist values which had come to dominate Khmer society by the time of its final composition, the *Reamker* is a uniquely Khmer invention.

This early literary text is thought, moreover, to have been a sort of libretto for dramatic performance. Two genres of Khmer dance practised today, *sbaek thom* (a kind of shadow theatre) and *lakhon khol* (an all-male dance–drama), are entirely dedicated to representation of episodes of this epic tale. The *Reamker* forms a central part of the repertoire of *lakhon preah reach troap* or *lakhon luong* (court or classical dance). Few dramatic representations today begin the story as in the classical text, that is, before the marriage of Rama (Preah Ream in Khmer) and Sita (Neang Seda). The *Reamker* opens instead episodes later where we see Preah Ream accompanied by his wife Neang Seda and brother Laksmana (Preah Leak) wandering in exile from their homeland. The ogre King Ravana (Reab) abducts Neang Seda, inciting the epic battle—a long series of battles—between the ogres and Preah Ream's monkey army, headed by the monkey warrior Hanuman. The eventual victory of the princes and the retrieval of Neang Seda is followed by another long series of tribulations primarily concerning the royal couple. Episodes following the great battle are however less frequently represented in dramatic performance today. As will be further described in the following chapters, *sbaek thom*, *lakhon khol*, and *lakhon preah reach troap* each typically perform different scenes from the sequence outlined above, though there is of course thematic overlap in their respective repertoires.

Other arts find in the story unending inspiration. *Reamker* performances are associated with all kinds of religious practices today, including those specifically derived from animist beliefs. *Lakhon khol*, for example, is traditionally performed to ask the gods for rain, a quintessential animist rite.

8

Though Cambodia's rich written and iconographic evidence testifies to the pervasive importance of dance in ancient Cambodia, and provides clues to the origins of modern interpretation of tradition, it leaves us with little understanding of the types of dance performance known in past times. The sources offer, for example, nothing like the Indian *Natyashastra*, an analytical presentation of dramatic art. That dancers worked in the service of temples in pre-Angkorian and Angkorian times is a historical truth, but what exactly they danced remains something of a mystery. The *Reamker* text was written in the sixteenth or seventeenth century as a support for dramatic performance, but for exactly what kind of performance we do not know.

Some contemporary dance forms are thought to be derived from indigenous ritual. Others would seem to have Indian dance as a primary influence. Still others are thought to have been introduced to Cambodia from neighbouring cultures, some of which had already been 'Indianized' themselves. Yet to search for a single original source of Khmer dance is in many ways to miss the point, because each genre of Khmer dance constitutes a specific configuration of diverse influences over time.

Any understanding of the development of dance must take into consideration not only the remarkable continuation but also the repeated rupture of tradition. This is of course particularly true of arts for which there is no written support, where both the liberty and the limitations of the tradition are thereby heightened. In dance, it is the *dancing* and the *dancers* which constitute the archive assuring the perpetuation of tradition. This situation, where the performance and the archive of the tradition in many ways coincide, seems to lend itself at once to conservative and innovative possibilities of cultural transmission.

During what is known as the middle period of Cambodian history, stretching roughly from the time preceding the fall of Angkor in the fifteenth century to that preceding the establishment of the French Protectorate in the nineteenth, many of the cultural structures of today's Cambodia took form. We see in this time the earliest expression of a Theravadin culture assimilated with animism and nurtured by Brahmanic and Mahayanic tradition. The gradual

loss of political coherence and sovereignty Cambodia was to know in the middle period, and particularly from the seventeenth to the nineteenth centuries preceding the establishment of the French Protectorate, effected significant change in all domains. Change is not, however, to be summarily equated with loss. The Post-Angkorian period was to some extent characterized by increased contact with the outside world. The advent of Theravada Buddhism in the place of ancient Cambodia's primarily Brahmanic rule gave rise to new popular artistic expression, including the composition of the *Ramayana* in Khmer as mentioned above. New dance genres and musical ensembles would seem to have developed during this relatively tumultuous time. Radical rupture in tradition itself created a powerful drive for restoration of loss. And, as we witness in the modern period, the movement for restoration creates new tradition out of the old.

The first writings about Khmer dance as an art form date to the turn of the twentieth century after the establishment of the French Protectorate. This attention from the outside was itself to affect the evolution of the performing arts as French and Khmer authorities alike consciously attempted to revive tradition. A School of Arts was founded in Phnom Penh in 1919 with the mission of reinvigorating some of Cambodia's fine and craft arts. This was a precursor of the Conservatory of Performing Arts and the Royal University of Fine Arts, institutions developed in the 1950s and 1960s with the aim of fostering indigenous scholarship on the arts, including dance, in the wake of independence.

It was in the context of a 'Khmerization' of governmental structures and national education programmes that artists from the capital began to research regional and ethnic performance traditions. Some folk dances found in the countryside were reworked by professional artists, and reintroduced to the populations which had inspired them in the first place. In addition, depending on the shifting political winds over the course of this century, classical dance has been alternately removed from and restored to the control of the monarchy. Yet, even within the University or the Department of Performing Arts (which replaced the Conservatory in the 1980s), classical dance has remained in a sense aloof from its

secular supports. It is revered—or by some disdained—in its highly symbolic associations with royalty. None the less, displaced from their traditional settings in the court, the temple, or the village, dance genres taught at the University have been simultaneously preserved and transformed.

The wars of the 1970s and 1980s took an incalculable toll on the performing arts. Virtually all ritual and formal performance, as the Khmer had known them, came to a standstill during the Khmer Rouge period from 1975–9, when close to 2 million people perished from starvation, disease, forced labour, torture, and execution. The singular massacre of artists over those four years left all the arts severely crippled. Faced with the fragility of a tradition which has always been transmitted from master to disciple through long periods of apprenticeship, dance practitioners have shown great courage in recreating and reinvigorating their art.

This book aims to give the reader a general understanding of the major genres of dance and dance–drama practised in Cambodia today. Given the presence of dance in so many Khmer performing arts, any attempt at making absolute distinctions between dance and theatre proves impossible. On the contrary, as we will see, there is constant overlap between *robam*, the generic Khmer term for dance, and *lakhon*, generally translated as theatre. Several types of drama which incorporate structured movement patterns have not been included here, both because of space limitations and because they tend to emphasize dialogue and song over dance. Further, again because of space considerations, we have opted not to cover popular social dance in this book. Paradoxically, the very fact that dance is a fundamental component of most social and religious rites in Cambodia—ranging from possession ceremonies to marriage ritual to a myriad of Buddhist celebrations—prohibits detailed discussion of these various phenomena in this short volume. Some pictures are included, however, in view of suggesting their variety and amplitude (Colour Plates 3 and 4).

The book is organized according to genres as they are defined in Khmer tradition. Chapter 2 presents a form of shadow theatre (*sbaek thom*). Chapter 3 covers court or classical dance and dance–drama (*lakhon preah reach troap*, also known as *lakhon luong* or

robam boran). Chapter 4 treats all-male dance–drama (*lakhon khol*). Chapter 5 looks at folk dance (*robam propeiney*), which incorporates both ritual and theatrical forms, the latter codified at the Royal University of Fine Arts over recent decades.

The majority of the dance genres discussed are in one way or another ceremonial. Yet some of those which were once most closely associated with ritual are in modern practice most closely associated with tourism, admittedly a kind of ritual in itself. The genres presented in Chapters 2, 3, and 4 can in many ways be considered as variations on a single theme. They are primarily types of dance–drama relating episodes from the *Reamker*, though the classical repertoire also includes other mythico-historical tales, as well as pure dance pieces—discrete, relatively short works that do not tell a story but none the less communicate a sublime message.

For some of these genres, the setting is similar in that performance and audience areas seem to overlap. Yet while there may exist no physically delimited stage, the space is sacralized by a preliminary ritual. Virtually all performance is preceded by the *sampeah kru* ceremony through which participants ask various gods and local spirits as well as the spirits of deceased dance masters to help guide the artists. Accompanied by offerings of incense, candles, and various delicacies and accoutrements, these rituals help the dancers prepare to transpose themselves into the characters they are about to portray, and to elevate the performance above the everyday world in which it is, yet, firmly rooted.

In examining the movement style, musical and textual accompaniment, and performance framework of a given dance genre, we aim to place the dance in its cultural and historical contexts, while also pointing toward the more universal issues at hand. For instance, in Khmer dance we see clearly the tension between repetition and innovation characteristic of all artistic creation. As in any culture at any time, individual experience is expressed publicly through controlled, codified, and yet telling forms. Habitual ways of perceiving and understanding are shaken, confirmed, and renewed through dance performance. As an example, one might consider the various uses and representations of gender difference in Khmer dance. Some roles conform to a highly stylized typology,

with women dancers playing stereotypical 'female' parts and men dancers playing 'male' ones. Yet women play men in the almost all-female classical dance, men play women in the all-male *lakhon khol*, and mediums undergo multiple and spectacular transformations in trance. We are witness to the simultaneous delineation and transgression of sexual boundaries; the ostensibly incompatible cultural phenomena of perpetuation and innovation are conjugated in a single performance.

Many viewers unfamiliar with South-East or South Asia may find it difficult at first to appreciate the power of Khmer dance. This difficulty is due in general to the cultural distance involved, which a few pertinent remarks can help bridge. First, as mentioned above, the dance tradition is largely composed of dance–drama, the performance of stories well-known to Khmer spectators. Without the relevant cultural referents, much of the humour and tragedy is lost. Formal differences may also shake associations. Corporal movement is in general relatively restrained. Facial expression can be extremely subtle. The lack of distinction between performance and audience spaces in some contexts, along with the slow rhythm and long duration of much traditional performance, differ from the modern Western experience of theatre. It is in fact these very characteristics, combined with many other elements, which contribute to the performative illusion of entering another time and space. We hope that the information and descriptions provided in this book will help the outsider cross cultural borders—which at times can even be difficult to locate—and enter the world of Khmer dance.

Our choice of terminology reflects an attempt to strike a balance between the specificity of Khmer dance and the universal nature of the art. We have tried to remain faithful to Khmer conceptions of dance without overloading the reader with unfamiliar vocabulary. The English terms we employ are rarely direct translations of the Khmer, but instead represent our attempt to best capture the concept under discussion. In some cases it is the multiplicity of Khmer terms for one genre which prohibits direct translation. In others, it is the singularity of the Khmer. Court or classical dance, for example, gives a very general sense of what in Khmer is traditionally called *lakhon luong*, 'king's drama', or *lakhon preah reach troap*, 'drama

of royal heritage', and which political and cultural authorities in the capital have often called since the 1970s *robam boran*, 'ancient dance'. Because its origins may well have been as much in the temple as in the court, and because it is not strictly associated with royalty today, we have decided to call it both classical and court. *Lakhon khol*, on the other hand, is difficult to render directly into English because the origins and meaning of the term *khol* remain uncertain, such that *khol* functions as a proper name of one kind of *lakhon*. As the commonly employed English designation of *lakhon khol*, 'masked dance–drama' seems to us misleading—particularly given that in other genres such as classical dance some performers also wear masks—we have opted to call this performance genre 'all-male dance–drama'. Throughout the book, however, Khmer terms are also frequently employed in alternation with the English, and in view of recalling the 'proper' which any gloss may otherwise lead the reader to overlook.

With the exception of words which have entered into common English usage, such as Phnom Penh or Shiva, Khmer or Sanskrit terms used in modern Khmer are given in simplified phonetic transcription. A glossary gives the Khmer and a brief definition of all terms which figure in phonetic transcription in the text.

1. K. 286, George Cœdès *Inscriptions du Cambodge*, IV, Paris, Ecole Française d'Extrême-Orient, 1952, pp. 88–101.

2. Strictly speaking, the term Cambodian designates nationality, while the term Khmer refers to the ethnic group constituting the large majority of Cambodians. We have, however, chosen to follow common usage in employing the two terms interchangeably. Only in discussions concerning other ethnic groups in Cambodia do we use Khmer in its more specific ethnic sense.

3. K. 600, George Cœdès *Inscriptions du Cambodge*, II, Hanoi, Ecole Française d'Extrême-Orient, 1992, pp. 21–3.

2
Shadow Theatre

ONE evening in March 1997, two very different theatrical performances took place at the Bakong Temple in Siem Reap Province during a festival celebrating the cremation of a venerated monk: one was a modern stage play of an Indian love story, and the other was *sbaek thom*, a kind of shadow theatre. Before the performances, as the players of both troupes were preparing themselves and their sets on the temple grounds only a few hundred metres from each other, one of the stage actors commented about the rival production of shadow theatre: '*Sbaek thom* is the oldest, the most traditional kind of drama in Cambodia. In ancient times', he continued, 'people didn't dare to show their bodies to the public. First they used shadow puppets. Then they came out, but not all the way: they wore masks. Finally, they dared to truly act on stage.'

This analysis of the history of Khmer performing arts, which implies an evolution from *sbaek thom* to masked drama to modern stage acting, is far from scientific, and reflects the amicable competition between two companies that would be vying for the public's attention that night. Self-proclaimed guardians of ancient tradition, members of the *sbaek thom* troupe pointed out their own austere superiority relative to their somewhat gaudy neighbours. Their performance made explicit statements about moral and traditional order. The stage actors had no such lofty goals. They were there to please the public, to entertain.

Sbaek thom literally means 'large leather', and it connotes both a form of shadow theatre and the cut-out leather puppets or panels it employs; the latter are also known simply as *sbaek*, 'leather'. The 'ancient' nature typically attributed to *sbaek thom* in Cambodia, also called *nang sbaek*, is yet to be verified by hard documentation. The earliest mention known to date refers to similar performances at

the Siamese court in the fifteenth century. In fact, the word *nang* is Siamese for leather, a synonym of the Khmer *sbaek*. It is quite likely, however, that the Siamese trace indicates an earlier exchange of the art from Cambodia to nascent Siam.

Shadow theatre is in the broadest sense an ancient art, still practised throughout much of Asia and beyond, from China, to India, to Turkey, and Greece. Based on the projection of light and shadows by means of a luminous source, opaque panels or puppets manipulated by the players, and a translucent screen or curtain, shadow theatre functions through the apparition of figures that are at once immaterial and mysteriously captivating. While the exact origins and history of the Khmer *sbaek thom* tradition are elusive, the stage actors at Bakong Temple were no doubt correct in referring to the ancient nature of the art form itself.

The closest kin to the Khmer *sbaek thom* is the Thai *nang yai*, 'large leather (panels or puppets)'. Certain similarities in performance technique are found elsewhere as well, most notably in India, Indonesia, and Malaysia where we see, for example, comparable alternating structures of textual and musical arrangements in all three countries. However, it is a different form of Khmer shadow theatre, *sbaek touc*, 'small leather (puppets)', also known as *ayong*, which much more closely resembles those other neighbouring traditions.

Indeed, *sbaek thom* stands out for its uniqueness with respect to other forms of shadow theatre. As opposed to the relatively small puppets with articulated members used in most shadow theatre performance—of which the Javanese *wayang kulit* is perhaps the most elaborate and well known—the Khmer *sbaek thom* primarily employs large panels which incorporate one or more figures into a framed decor. These supple leather panels, measuring up to 1 square metre, are attached to one or two vertical wooden rods which lend support and, descending below the bottom of the panel, serve as handles with which the player manipulates the *sbaek* above his or her head. Also, unlike other traditions in which one master, such as the Javanese *dalang*, commands the entire performance as puppet manipulator and narrator, *sbaek thom* employs a full troupe of manipulators and narrators. Moreover, in that projection of the

puppets' or panels' shadows onto a screen is only one of its many modes of presentation, *sbaek thom* is not strictly or exclusively a shadow theatre. The *sbaek* can also be held against the front of the screen in such a way that the spectator actually sees the panels rather than their shadows. The panels can even be moved away from the screen, into the space before the audience.

But the most remarkable specificity of *sbaek thom* in relation to other shadow theatre traditions, specificity which justifies its inclusion in the present book, is indeed dance. *Sbaek thom* is also dance–drama. The players are dancers—their bodies move along with, and one might say as extensions of the figures they animate. In this way the puppets are made to 'dance' as well.

Sbaek thom forms a continuum with Khmer classical dance and *lakhon khol*, discussed in the following chapters. As mentioned in the introduction, the repertoire of each draws from the *Reamker*. Indeed, *sbaek thom* and *lakhon khol* perform *only* episodes from this epic tale. Together, they evince a common aesthetic of composition and decor which would seem to take the famous stone reliefs of ancient temples such as Angkor Vat as a central and continuing point of reference. The figures cut in leather suggest postures similar to those of classical and *khol* dancers (Plate 22). Character features are codified in an analogous manner, such that from one genre to the next an ogre is immediately recognizable as an ogre, a prince as a prince. With his or her lower body, the *sbaek* dancer also moves in ways reminiscent of classical dance and *khol* where, for the most part, knees are bent, toes are flexed, and thighs retain a constant turnout.

Each of these three genres also maintains a reference to court tradition, be it in some cases only vestigial. Though in provincial areas today it is firmly linked to the popular setting of the Buddhist temple, *sbaek thom* is sometimes qualified by the term *luong*, 'king' or 'royal'. Ever since the earliest surviving unambiguous documentation of the genre in the nineteenth century, its most revered practitioners, those considered to be its most authentic masters, have come from Siem Reap province, the seat of the Angkorian Empire from the ninth to the fifteenth centuries. *Sbaek thom* troupes also thrived at the sites of subsequent royal capitals, Oudong and Phnom

22. The action of flying is depicted in this *sbaek* as in classical
dance and *lakhon khol* with one leg bent and lifted to the
back, sole facing the sky. (Deth Sovutha)

Penh, as well as in Battambang, an important cultural centre where much royal tradition was appropriated by provincial authorities particularly in the nineteenth and early twentieth centuries.

Two full *sbaek thom* troupes, both all male, were maintained in Cambodia in the first half of the twentieth century, one in Battambang, the other in Siem Reap. In the 1960s, students at the Royal University of Fine Arts studied under Siem Reap masters to create a shortened version for outdoor or stage performance. Full *sbaek* sets, composed of more than 150 panels and puppets, were held by these two provincial troupes. In the early 1970s, the Siem Reap set was transferred to Phnom Penh for safekeeping. Most but not all of the original Siem Reap *sbaek* survived the war. The Battambang set has, however, reputedly been lost.

The effects of turbulent recent history on this performance tradition are still tangible. Loss in human and material resources over the course of the 1970s was great. Transmission of the art from master to disciple was interrupted not only during the Khmer Rouge period but also for years thereafter as surviving players lacked the material means to reconstitute their troupes and their *sbaek* sets. The relatively high production cost of *sbaek thom* panels, which has undoubtedly always limited expansion of the art in the rural setting, proves virtually prohibitive in Cambodia's present economic context. As each large *sbaek* is made from a single cowhide, more than 150 cows are needed to constitute a set. This requires a significant investment on the part of the community whose contributions are typically collected through the Buddhist temple.

Performances are traditionally sponsored by a community as part of collective celebrations. Before the war in Siem Reap, the *sbaek thom* troupe was systematically hired to perform on temple grounds or in an adjoining field at the New Year, at the annual Celebration of the Dead, and at the cremation of important religious figures. The performance would generally last for seven successive nights. Though its ritual role is much less specific than that of *lakhon khol* described in Chapter 4, its powers conceived in less explicitly magical terms, *sbaek thom* can also be performed in view of combating natural calamities such as a drought or an epidemic. In this

context, the performance is offered to the divinities as a kind of appeasement. The enactment of the epic tale constitutes an homage to the gods it depicts, and aims to elevate its participants, players and spectators alike, out of their ordinary lives to a higher order.

The weakening of the fabric of Khmer society, which has largely resulted from recent wars and is not unrelated to persistent rural poverty, continues to threaten the survival of this art so closely associated with traditional community structures. Ceremonies which would once have been sponsored by the local community are now frequently sponsored by an individual or single family, often from the city or abroad. In this new economic arrangement, villagers and temple leaders are engaged to prepare the ceremony to be held in their village and, to a certain extent, for their benefit, but they relinquish their right to join in overall organizational planning. Local artists and performance traditions are frequently overlooked in the process. Projection of Chinese or Indian videos has become an economical substitute for live performance. When live performance is commissioned, other traditional theatre forms are often easier to find than *sbaek thom*.

None the less, *sbaek thom* has survived. Teaching groups of disciples from Siem Reap, Battambang, and Phnom Penh, a few Siem Reap masters, along with their families and other remaining troupe members, have played a key role in reviving the art. Young artists are trained in the specific elements which compose *sbaek thom*: leather carving, panel manipulation, dance, recitation, and music. Under the direction of one of the old masters, Ty Chean, the prewar Siem Reap troupe has been partly reconstituted. With support from international aid agencies, new troupes of *sbaek thom* or *sbaek touc* have also been established in both provinces. The Ministry of Culture's Department of Performing Arts recreated a Phnom Penh-based *sbaek thom* troupe in the 1980s. This group of performers, consisting of about fifteen *sbaek* dancers, appears at ceremonies, in theatrical shows featuring various kinds of music and dance, and in national and international festivals. Ty Chean's Siem Reap troupe also sometimes performs at such national venues. Ceremonial performances are less frequent for all troupes than in the pre-war era, and rarely last the full seven nights. A further significant, and

perhaps lasting, change undergone by *sbaek thom* in the past decades is the introduction of female players into the performance tradition.

Performance Framework

Sbaek thom is traditionally performed in the open air with no raised stage. The performance space is centred around the screen—a white cloth, which can measure more than 10 metres in length and 5 metres in height, stretched between two vertical poles.[1] A small platform made of banana tree trunks holds the bonfire a metre or so behind the centre of the screen. This light source which allows shadows to be cast onto the screen is often now replaced or complemented by electric or neon bulbs. The 'backstage' area is demarcated by a thatched barrier erected in a semi-circle another few metres back and centred roughly on the fire. The *sbaek* are grouped together by episode and propped up against this structure before the performance. It is in this space, quite open to public view, that performers prepare themselves and await their turn on 'stage'. The behind-the-scene show in fact attracts numerous spectators. Over the course of a performance, many people move from the space reserved for the audience in front to crowd around the openings between the ends of the screen and the thatch semi-circle to view the puppets, the dancers, and the fire from behind.

A symmetrical semi-circular space is also informally delimited in front of the screen. This is the performance area, with outer boundaries defined by the audience and by the *pin peat* orchestra musicians seated on mats a few metres away from the screen.

A performance opens well after sunset with a *sampeah kru* ritual through which homage is paid to the principal divinities, Buddha, Shiva and Vishnu, the god of Fire, the patron gods of the arts, diverse protective spirits and ancestral masters, as well as certain characters in the performance. In preparation for this opening rite, puppets representing the most important characters from a ritual point of view are propped up against the front of the screen. These include the mythical sage and ancestral guardian of performance arts, Maha Eysei, in the centre, usually flanked by Shiva, Preah

21

Ream, and sometimes Reab. Candles attached to each displayed figure are lit. Offerings are placed at their feet, in the orchestra space, and on the raised bonfire platform behind the screen. Dressed simply in white shirts, coloured *kben* (traditional pantaloons), with a coloured sash at the waist, the players line up in a V-shape in the performance space in front of the screen. With their backs turned to the orchestra and the audience, they squat and raise their hands in prayer. Invocations to the divinities are chanted in low tones with musical accompaniment. The ritual comes to a dramatic conclusion as the fire behind the screen is lit and the narrators, followed by all the players, let out three abrupt cries in unison—as if to scare off evil spirits, and very often jolting the audience too.

After this ritual opening, a theatrical prelude with a highly symbolic moral content sets the tone for the night's epic narration. Two monkeys, one white and the other black, enter into combat. Victorious, the white monkey brings his captive to the old sage Maha Eysei for judgement. On their way to the hermitage, the monkeys come upon a group of village men. The encounter between mythical monkey warriors and humble villagers in this opening scene, through which a 'real' comic world meets an epic and tragic one, serves in a symbolic way to draw the spectators into the struggle between good and evil. In the ensuing comical scene which is partially improvised, references are made to the actual ceremonial and performance setting. Moreover, the self-denigrating comic relief provided by these village characters intermittently during the performance implicates the spectators throughout the legendary narrative. At performances staged by the Phnom Penh troupe in Paris in 1997, for example, the players used broken French in a chain of bilingual wordplays. At the Bakong performance mentioned above, the initial encounter between monkeys and villagers was set on that temple's grounds.

After a series of crafty linguistic dodges in response to the monkey's request to meet Maha Eysei, the buffoonish and initially reticent villagers finally lead them to the wise man. Maha Eysei calms the crowd, but refuses to condemn the black monkey. 'You are only different colours of the same race', he says. 'You must

show solidarity. One day you will together serve our worthy savior.' Maha Eysei's judgement, which has prefaced *sbaek thom* performances for decades and very likely centuries, carries a message of uncanny pertinence in today's Cambodia. He orders the white monkey to set the black monkey free, and appeals to the two to settle their differences by non-violent means.

The sequence of episodes most frequently performed in *sbaek thom* is known as the Battle of Indrajit. One of the many battles making up the great war between Preah Ream's and Reab's armies, the story is itself composed of a series of conflicts between troupes led by Indrajit, who is Reab's warrior son, and the Prince's army. The sequence begins with the construction by Preah Ream's army of a bridge to Lanka, Reab's island kingdom. Over the course of the narration, we see the combatants of either side in strategical planning sessions, in celebration, in meditation, or in mourning. These behind-the-lines scenes alternate with others depicting the confrontation of the two sides, confrontation in which military might is inevitably second to magical ruse. One episode recounting the transformation of Reab's niece Punyakay into Seda is among the most popular within the Indrajit sequence today. At her uncle's order, Punyakay takes the form of the corpse of Seda, Preah Ream's abducted wife, floating on the water before Preah Ream's camp. The stratagem has its intended effect when Preah Ream, holding the body of Punyakay–Seda in his arms, falls unconscious. However, Hanuman, Preah Ream's monkey-general, suspects foul play and orders the corpse to be burned. Punyakay escapes from the flames, and, flying into the sky, is caught by Hanuman. The impersonator is tortured, raped, and abandoned by her monkey captors. Other equally unsettling war crimes are played out until Indrajit, decapitated, finally meets his end.

The fact that this and other episodes performed in *sbaek thom* can also be found in *lakhon khol* performance, but do not figure in the classical sixteenth-century *Reamker* text, raises interesting questions regarding the role of dramatic performance in cultural innovation and preservation. Certain variations on the *Ramayana* tale which have not survived in the classical text may well have been developed and/or preserved through performance. The *Reamker*

archive is as much within the minds and bodies of performers as on the written page.

The Leather Panels

The leather figures are works of art in themselves. Their craftsmen must not only command multiple techniques specific to leather-work but must also demonstrate skill in traditional drawing. First, a complete design is drawn in chalk on a tanned cowhide. Holes are then chiselled out of the cowhide according to this design. The leather-worker must remove small pieces of leather which will let light through while maintaining the structural integrity of the panel. As shadow theatre is based on the contrast between light areas of the illuminated screen and dark areas where light is blocked by the leather, there are two general techniques of representation available to the leather-worker. Either the main elements of the figure (body parts and others) are cut out of the leather panel to leave the figure mostly light against a mostly dark background within the frame of the panel, or else the opposite is done, to give a dark figure against a mostly light ground. The first technique is usually used for faces and upper bodies of noble and sometimes ogre women. With only a thin leather outline left to distinguish features, the women appear white-skinned and delicate. The leather in certain areas of some female figures can also be shaved thin to further enhance the passage of light. The second technique is invariably used for male figures (Plates 23 and 24).

Gender, action, and emotion all figure in the codification of panel design. Princes and ogres are, for example, almost invariably represented in profile. Women are presented frontally. Traditional gestures and postures are immutable. The set of puppets used for a given episode is also more or less fixed. Though faithful reproduc-tion of tradition is the rule, each artist's personal style can be seen in small details of design. New panels are also periodically created to respond to new choreographic needs.

Ritual practices are involved in the fabrication and subsequent care of a number of the figures, above all Maha Eysei, who are considered to bear supernatural powers. According to some artists,

24

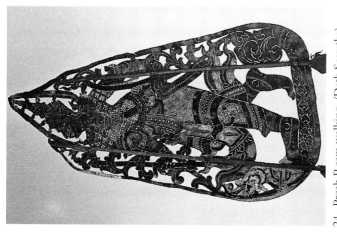

24. Preah Ream walking. (Deth Sovutha)

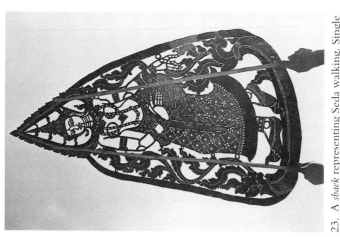

23. A *sbaek* representing Seda walking. Single characters are often presented within more triangular or tear-drop shaped panels such as this one. (Deth Sovutha)

the Maha Eysei puppet is to be completed between sunrise and sunset of one day. It is displayed on an altar between performances, and always kept separately from the other puppets when transported or preceding performance.

The panels are remarkable graphic compositions. Most are in fact framed by a border sculpted into the general composition. Many of the larger panels are more or less rectangular in shape with rounded corners. They can contain a single character within a complex floral decor. The character can also be depicted in an architectural setting, riding an animal mount, or in a drawn chariot with a charioteer and other servants or companions. The different elements—human, animal, and vegetal—are associated in form and decor to form a continuum of movement very much like that seen on Angkorian reliefs.

The panels can also depict whole scenes rather than just individual characters. We see, for example, birds preying on the corpse of Punyakay–Seda floating on the waves (Plate 25). Another panel

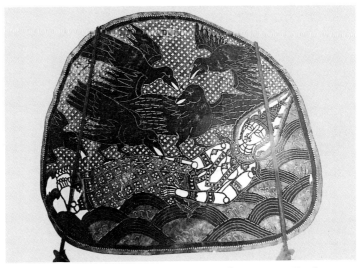

25. Punyakay transformed into Seda floating on the water near Preah Ream's camp. (Deth Sovutha)

from this same episode shows Preah Ream cradling the corpse (Plate 26); a flame-like decor rises above the united figures, suggesting the confused passion and tragedy of the scene. Numerous characters can be represented together, entangled, for example, in combat. Only a few figures are not framed. These include the smaller comical village characters and monkey foot-soldiers (Colour Plate 5).

As mentioned, the puppets are displayed in a variety of ways. They are moved across the back of the screen such that their shadows are projected onto the screen for the audience seated on the other side. Moved across the front of the screen they are also viewed directly (Colour Plates 6 and 7). During certain dance

26. Preah Ream cradling what he believes to be Seda's corpse.
(Deth Sovutha)

interludes, performers manipulate the puppets while performing in the space between the screen and the seated audience (Colour Plate 8).

A series of panels is deployed to enact any given sequence. A combat scene can make use, for example, of two or more panels first representing the enemy parties as separate figures. Combat can be simulated by overlapping two figures in movement. The panels are made to struggle against each other. As conflict heightens, however, the individual figure panels are replaced by another panel representing the two or more combatants entangled in a single composition. In the Punyakay episode outlined above, at one moment both the panel representing Punyakay–Seda floating in the waters and another representing Preah Ream at his camp are displayed on the screen (Plate 27). After Preah Ream has recognized his dead wife, these are replaced by a single panel representing the two characters together (see Plate 26).

Narration, Music, and Movement

The visual aspects of *sbaek thom* are inseparable from their aural counterparts as shifts in narrative mode and/or musical accompaniment serve to signal panel changes. The overall rhythm and balance of the performance is in fact typically ensured by two narrators who stand primarily at either end of the screen to describe the scene, recount the action, engage in dialogue, and command melodies from the orchestra. Arranging each of the elements which make up *sbaek thom* into a harmonious whole, they are in a sense the composers of each night's performance. Moreover, as they convey emotion through vocal, facial, and bodily expression, the narrators are important actors in the drama. They may also enter the action in front of the screen, and even dance with the panels.

The narration is composed of a number of different verse and prose styles. In one verse form, the narrators alternate in reciting stanzas. The drums, which are dramatically sounded at the conclusion of each stanza, signal the change in narrator. In other styles, alternation is by scene or character. One scene is presented by one

27. At his camp, Preah Ream sees Punyakay–Seda's body floating on the water. (Deth Sovutha)

narrator; the next scene by the other. Or, representing two different characters, the two narrators can engage in poetic or prose dialogue. Pure music pieces also alternate with recitation, with such shifts marked by drum beats or rolls as well.

The general horizontal movement from one end of the screen to the other is reinforced in *sbaek thom* by this aural accompaniment as the audience is constantly shifting its attention right and left. The

29

narrative tension between two contending camps, first presented in the monkey prelude and then in the Battle of Indrajit, is built up through these intertwined dramatic techniques.

Many scenes open with one or more puppets held immobile against the back or the front of the screen. The narrators present the setting, characters, and general situation. When action or dialogue begins, the dancers move the puppets accordingly. At the meeting between Reab and Punyakay for example, the ogre king looks down from his palace onto his frightened niece. The narrator takes on an authoritative stance to give Reab's orders. Slight movement of the panel signals that Reab is speaking. When responding for Punyakay, the narrator is notably demure. The Punyakay figure inclines forward in subservience. The drums sound, introducing a change in scene. After a brief melody, the narrator describes the scene of Punyakay near Preah Ream's camp. Her thoughts are voiced as her figure is displayed. This Punyakay panel is then replaced by another representing Seda as the narrator recounts the metamorphosis. Music finally replaces recitation as we see the panel representing Punyakay–Seda's body floating on the water. Dancer and panel undulate with the waves, moving slowly first across the back and then along the front of the screen. The dancer crosses the right leg over the left, then shifts his or her weight to the left leg in taking a step left, all the while pulling the panel (initially held up with one straight and one bent arm) downward in a measured gesture. The panel then rides a wave upwards as the dancer steps with right leg behind the left, taps the right leg even further to the back and, with the torso initiating the turn of head and hips, starts travelling anew. Pure music and dance passages such as this one come as a kind of release from scenes of encounter presented through recitation and more subtle movement.

Like the panel he or she displays, the dancer's body is also seen against the screen. As mentioned earlier, movement continues into the dancer's lower body as he or she enacts the role of the character or the action of the scene displayed. *Sbaek* dancers demonstrate the same sprightliness of a monkey, high-gaited vigour of an ogre, constrained grace of a female, and refined force of a male character as do classical or *khol* dancers. However, since movement is largely

restricted to the horizontal plane, with arms and hands engaged in manipulating heavy puppets, the gestural qualities of *sbaek* are necessarily somewhat unique.

Periodically, the dancers break away from the screen, into the space in front of the audience as mentioned earlier. For example, combat scenes in which opposing panels may overlap at times to simulate the violence of the battle can suddenly burst in this way into full dance pieces. Holding the panels up against each other, the dancers perform the combat in three dimensions. Certain scenes are moreover enacted directly by the dancers who leave their panels or puppets propped against the front of the screen to incarnate the characters represented.

Sbaek thom's reference to Angkorian sculpture far exceeds formal imitation of motifs and themes or sentimental recollection of a lost past. The reference, which can be seen to varying degrees in a number of Khmer performance genres, is indeed fundamental in both structural and conceptual terms to *sbaek thom*, where the visual rendering of narrative reflects the presentation of Angkorian reliefs with particular precision. The second-level, concentric enclosure–gallery of Angkor Vat, which displays narratives horizontally, provides a remarkable model for comparison. As in every *sbaek thom* performance, along the galleries of Angkor Vat, majestic processions alternate with combat or other scenes depicting encounters between allies or enemies, between leaders and subjects. Epic characters and events are associated with the familiar of everyday life as musicians play and monkeys tumble. It is thought that, like the murals painted on the inner walls of the enclosure–gallery of Phnom Penh's Royal Palace, Angkor Vat's sculpted galleries were designed to be open, at least periodically, to the public, and that viewing the narrative reliefs through circumambulation constituted a sort of edifying and purifying ritual for ancient pilgrims to this temple, a ritual enjoyed anew by appreciative tourists today. At Angkor Vat, the Battle of Lanka is thus brought to life as the viewer moves through the gallery. *Sbaek thom* produces a similar effect of animating the inanimate—only the *sbaek* viewer remains in a fixed position while the carved panels move across the illuminated screen. It is through the public act of

devotion—walking through the galleries, or attending a *sbaek* performance—that the epic comes to life. The re-enactment serves simultaneously to drive away evil spirits and to elevate human spirits.

Sbaek thom carries a distinctly religious and fundamentally ethical message. Good and evil, it teaches, coexist in an interminable dialectic. The Battle of Indrajit is repeatedly played out *because* the higher judgement, the verdict of the wise man Maha Eysei at the beginning of every performance, is not one of condemnation but rather of reconciliation. The subsequent drama constantly demonstrates the good within evil and the evil within good. We pity the ogre father mourning his dead son. We question the noble nature of a prince who shoots the fatal arrow into the enemy only when his back is turned. We are moved by the image of Seda floating lifeless on the ocean, by the grace and beauty of the scene, ominous echoes of the mortal nature of Preah Ream's doomed wife. We are moved even though we know it is only a death simulated by Punyakay within the simulation of the *sbaek thom* performance. Though the princes win out at the end of the play, in reality the dialectic continues. The sage refuses to consecrate the victory of good over evil, and calls instead for solidarity between conflicting forces. As the spectator is drawn into the drama, distinctions between the real and the legendary fade, and the battle starts again.

1. In contemporary performance a band of dark cloth can be attached to the bottom portion of the screen from around waist- to ground-level. Introduced by Phnom Penh-based arts researchers in the 1960s, this lower part of the screen is meant to lessen the distraction caused by puppet changes and other behind-the-screen activity.

3
Court/Classical Dance and Dance–Drama

LOOKING to ancient bas-reliefs for inspiration, court dance masters in the mid-twentieth century created a piece entitled *Apsara*. Surrounded by four or six dancers crowned with elaborate golden head-dresses, the central figure—the *apsara* Mera, one legendary founder of Cambodia—leads her coterie on an outing to a delectable garden. They delight in the beauty of the flowers, as the chorus sings of stringing tresses of the scented blossoms.

On stage the lights are raised just slightly, barely revealing the dancers. They stand across the back of the stage, facing forward, completely still, with one hand raised to eye level, palm reaching to the sky, elbow bent. The other hand is at waist level, fingers fanning backward. The *apsara* in the centre emerges into the spotlight, as if stepping out of a stone niche. In her skin-coloured body suit, skirt of shimmering brocade, and elaborate brass jewellery modelled on that worn by the *apsaras* of Angkorian reliefs, she brings the stone images to life. To the accompaniment of a *pin peat* ensemble, Mera approaches centre stage.

She performs a solo, facing one side and then the other. Her slow controlled movement is highly energized; toes and fingers are flexed, the back is arched. Her head moves in an almost imperceptible figure-eight wave. Her gaze reaches to the audience and beyond.

Mera is then joined by the other dancers, two or three on each side (Plate 28). At one point they lower themselves to the floor, resting one knee forward, and the other behind. With the rear foot flexed, sole to the sky, they are flying through the heavens, embodying a recollection of their Angkorian ancestors (Plate 29).

28. The *Apsara* Dance performed in the Chan Chhaya Pavilion, Royal Palace, by dancers of the University of Fine Arts, 1992. (Toni Samantha Phim)

From beneath wide velvet belts decorated with brass bangles, they pull out golden flowers, and offer them to Mera. As the dance finishes, they glide upstage where they resume their original places, assuming their original attitude. They have retreated to the wall of rock.

The *Apsara* Dance was created for the modern stage out of an ancient tradition. While it is not overtly ritual in nature, by exploiting the deliberate and subtle flow of movement in the classical tradition, the dance maintains an intense ritual-like atmosphere. The formalized yet fleeting poses of classical dance recall the virtuosity of Angkorian sculptors in representing figures in space. The *Apsara* Dance, in its explicit reference to Angkor Vat's bas-reliefs, gives body to an association latent in all classical dance, that is, the tension between earthly groundedness and ethereal lightness evinced in a strong vertical pull, weight low and centred, balanced by movement across a horizontal plane. Sustained physical energy, visible in flexed fingers and toes and measured gestural progression,

34

29. Stone relief of flying *apsara* from the east gallery of Angkor Vat, 1991. Note similarity to representation of flight in Plate 22. (Toni Samantha Phim)

combines with fluid and seemingly effortless execution of posture and travel through space to convey at once a sense of solidity and of delicacy. With choreography based on circular patterns which some associate with the shape and movement of a mythical sacred serpent, the *naga*, no hard angles are traced by the dancers as they cross the floor.

Queen Sisowath Kossamak Nearyrath, Norodom Sihanouk's mother, was the inspiration behind the genesis of the *Apsara* Dance in the 1950s.[1] Sihanouk's daughter, Princess Norodom Buppha Devi, was the first star of this dance. With the Queen's use of the images of celestial dancers on ancient temple walls as portraits of the forebearers of Cambodia's earthly dancers, she was seen to perpetuate a long tradition.

Characters and Repertoire

Classical or court dances and dance–dramas include a host of characters. The four main types are the gentle princess or female deity, the noble prince or male deity, the forceful ogre (giant), and the spry monkey. All but the monkeys and clown or hermit characters are played by women.

Most princesses or celestial women appear in tight-fitting bodices which are sleeveless on the right side. A sequinned sash is draped over the left shoulder. A pleated brocade skirt falls just above the ankles which are adorned with thick brass bracelets. Strands of jasmine blossoms dangle over the left ear to grace a golden tiara. A flower in full bloom is placed behind the other ear (Colour Plate 9).

The princes and male deities wear slightly higher crowns. Their long-sleeved sequinned tops are adorned with pointed epaulets. They wear tight-fitting pants which come to just below the knee as a first layer, over which a 3-metre length of brocade is wrapped, twisted, and pulled through the legs to make elaborately pleated pantaloons. Jewellery for the male characters is intricate, just as it is for the females.[2] Until the middle of the twentieth century with the introduction of Western make-up, dancers painted their faces white, lending an other-worldliness to their art.

1. Im Chil, one of Cambodia's last remaining traditional gong makers at work. Rejecting modern methods in which molten metal is poured into moulds, this artisan, assisted by members of his extended family, uses traditional tools to beat the hot metal into the ancient knobbed form, Phnom Penh, 1994. (Ashley Thompson)

2. Twelfth-century sandstone bas-relief representing Rama carried by his monkey general Hanuman in the Battle of Lanka. This is a small segment from the sculpted galleries measuring more than half a kilometre in length and forming the second enclosure of Angkor Vat, 1995. (Ashley Thompson)

3. Medium in trance at Vat Run, Banteay Srei district, Siem Reap. The man is possessed by a local female spirit reputed to reside in the ruins of an ancient brick temple on the modern temple grounds, 1996. (Ashley Thompson)

4. A *chhayam* troupe leads a parade during a money-raising ceremony for a local temple, Kandal Province, 1990. (Toni Samantha Phim)

5. Encounter between monkeys and villagers, with Maha Eysei approaching from the far right of the screen, Bakong Temple, 1997. (Ang Chouléan)

6. Varied uses of shadow and light animate this *sbaek thom* scene in which the dancer with the large puppet *(left)* remains behind the screen, while the other puppeteers are in front of the screen. Performed by troupes from Siem Reap and the Department of Performing Arts, Phnom Penh, 1996. (Toni Samantha Phim)

7. The puppeteer holds a panel in front of the screen. *Sbaek thom* performance in Siem Reap, 1967. (Alain Daniel)

8. Dancers manipulating puppets in the performance space in front of the screen. The face and upper body of the female puppet is painted white to produce an effect of lightness when displayed in front of the screen. Such *sbaek* can function both as regular puppets and as shadow puppets, illuminated at once from the front and the back. Bakong Temple, 1997. (Ang Chouléan)

9. Dancers of the female role from the Department of Performing Arts perform the classical Blessing Dance in full costume in front of Angkor Vat, 1992. (Toni Samantha Phim)

10. The embroidering of costumes is a painstaking process in which specific designs are reproduced in layers of sequins, 1991. (Toni Samantha Phim)

11. Preah Ream (danced by Pen Sok Chea), followed by Neang Seda and Preah Leak, in the forest in a scene from the *Reamker*. Performed in Kompong Som by the Ministry of Culture's Department of Performing Arts, 1991. (Toni Samantha Phim)

12. Neang Seda (Ouk Soly Chumnit) undergoes a trial by fire. Royal
Dance Troupe, Pocheny Pavilion, Royal Palace, 1999. (Toni
Samantha Phim)

13. Dancers from the dance school affiliated with the University of Fine Arts, dressed as Doves of Peace, lead the parade during a national holiday marking the liberation of Phnom Penh from the Khmer Rouge, 1991. (Toni Samantha Phim)

14. Performances of many types of theatre and dance were extremely popular in the refugee and displaced persons camps established along the Thai–Cambodian border during the 1980s and early 1990s. (Tor Vutha, Site 2 Khmer Displaced Persons Camp, 1992; Courtesy of Association Phare)

15. Students of the University of Fine Arts dance school practise the core postures and movements of classical dance in the Chan Chhaya Pavilion of the Royal Palace. Those studying the female role wear red *kben* while those training to dance male or ogre roles wear blue during class, 1991. (Toni Samantha Phim)

16. Rows of multilevel banana trunk offerings lead to the altar holding masks and other dance paraphernalia in a *sampeah kru* ceremony presided over by Proeung Chhieng, a dean and dance teacher at the University of Fine Arts, 1991. (Toni Samantha Phim)

17. The *sampeah* gesture in dance is a refined version of a general Cambodian expression of greeting and respect, 1991. (Toni Samantha Phim)

18. Phka Soy, *lakhon khol* dance and recitation master, at his home in Svay Andet. The last living archive of the textual tradition, he is pictured here during a recording session with researchers from Phnom Penh's Buddhist Institute and the Royal University of Fine Arts' Department of Archeology. He died before completing recordings of the entire text, 1996. (Thonevath Pou)

19. *Lakhon khol* mask of an ogre surounded by offerings on an altar at the Svay Andet Temple superior's residence, Svay Andet village, Kandal Province, 1995. (Ashley Thompson)

20. Two *lakhon khol* dancers performing before a medium (older man in white) during the *sampeah kru* ceremony preceding the New Year's performance in Svay Andet village, 1995. (Ang Chouléan)

21. Preparing for a confrontation with the monkeys, this *lakhon khol* ogre assumes an assertive stance in the Battle at Night. Performed by Thavro Phim of the University of Fine Arts troupe on the grounds of the Royal Palace, 1992. (Toni Samantha Phim)

22. *Trot* performed during the New Year by dancers of the Department of Performing Arts in the Royal Palace compound, 1992. (Toni Samantha Phim)

23. Yim Sinath of the Department of Performing Arts in the
    Cardamom Picking Dance. Performed on the grounds of the
    Bassac Theatre, Phnom Penh, 1993. (Nop Bunna)

Ogres and monkeys always appear in masks specific to their character roles. Their long-sleeved tops are decorated with distinguishing designs embroidered in sequins (Colour Plate 10). Ogres have epaulets like the princes, while the monkeys have a short tail, fashioned from sequinned cloth and tipped with golden threads, which hangs down from under a wide embroidered belt.

The repertoire is composed of dance–dramas representing certain sequences from the *Reamker*, other mythico-historical tales and stories of the lives of the Buddha, as well as exclusively ceremonial dances, and new, shorter pieces. Selections are made from older as well as more recently created works for staged performances today. The *Apsara* Dance often greets the audience when the curtain first opens. The concluding number is frequently a sequence from the *Reamker* (Colour Plate 11). The story begins with Preah Ream, Preah Leak, and Neang Seda strolling through the forest, and picks up dramatic tension when Seda is abducted by Reab. He had approached her disguised as a hermit after she had sent Preah Ream off in pursuit of a golden deer, and then Preah Leak off in search of her husband. Some of the many adventures which ensue as Preah Ream enlists his monkey army to wage war against Reab and his ogre nation are then represented. The sequence can conclude with the return home of the victorious princes, bearing their precious bounty, Seda. Sometimes, however, we see a subsequent episode in which Seda, after being accused of infidelity by Preah Ream, is made to undergo a trial by fire, which she also survives (Colour Plate 12).

Stereotyped ideals of social behaviour are communicated in the pure dance as well as in the narrative pieces. The shyness, gentleness, and intelligence prized in women, and the strength and bravery of men are all recognizable through gesture, story, and facial expression to a Khmer audience. Yet these stereotypes are nuanced even as they are acted out. The noble men, in contrast to the giants, are gentle, even effeminate, while the noble females, with Seda as the prime example, prove themselves at times braver than their masculine counterparts. This blurring or vacillation of binary divisions is also manifest in narrative development as themes of justice and injustice, light and dark, beauty and ugliness introduce

reality into the very ideal world they project. There are, for example, few noble characters, such as Seda, beyond reproach. And the 'evil' characters inevitably have some sympathetic qualities.

The *pin peat* orchestra accompanies all classical dance, with a chorus singing poetic narration. Slow, high-pitched recitation interlaces with the piercing sound of the *sralai* (oboe). The *sampho* (drum), believed to contain powerful spirits, provides the accents for the timing of dance movements while the xylophones and gongs offer fluid elaborations on the melody. Hand-held wood or bamboo clackers sometimes used by the chorus add rhythmic emphasis.

History

In the nineteenth century, and after centuries of political instability, King Ang Duong (ruled 1841–60) largely succeeded in restoring national unity. His legacy, which included legal reform, infrastructure development, and rehabilitation of the court, prepared the ground for the establishment of the French Protectorate in 1863. Twentieth-century rulers, especially Norodom Sihanouk, regard Ang Duong as the founder of the modern Cambodian state, and have credited this monarch with initiating changes to Khmer court dance on the basis of Angkor Vat's twelfth-century *apsara* carvings.

Throughout the nineteenth and early twentieth centuries, royal dancers lived a secluded life inside the palace walls, practising daily, and serving and performing for the king (Plate 30). Palace performances primarily took place in the context of royal rituals such as a coronation, marriage, funeral, or the cutting of the topknot, a ceremony in which the tuft of hair which has been allowed to grow long atop a child's head is shaved off, signalling the passage into puberty. Under the French Protectorate, performances meant as entertainment were staged in the palace for visiting dignitaries. Some of these performances were in fact open to the public. However, the dancers, also often consorts of the monarch, emerged from the palace rarely, going out only when called upon to dance during rituals held in auspicious locations around Cambodia. On these occasions dance was a fundamental part of prayers addressed to the deities for the fertility and well-being of the country. The

30. Dancers in full costume demonstrate their art in the Chan Chhaya Pavilion
of the Royal Palace in the 1920s. (Courtesy of Missions Etrangères, Paris)

dance, and the dancers, were core elements in the ruler's symbolic
display of prowess.

Travellers and colonial authorities around the end of the nineteenth century noted the existence of classical dance troupes in
provincial settings, far from the royal court. In many cases a retired
palace dancer was the troupe's teacher. The performers were farmers
by trade, and practised when time permitted. Their costumes were
far less spectacular than those of their palace counterparts, yet their
performances drew from the same repertoire.

And, as they most probably did in ancient times, certain court
dignitaries or government officials also kept dance troupes. The
governor of north-western Battambang Province, for example, had
both female and male troupes reputedly modelled after court troupes.
Though Battambang, along with Siem Reap Province, was at the
time under Siamese control, and political tribute was thus paid to
the Siamese king, cultural references to the Khmer court remained
powerful. Oral histories of this governor's reign reveal the dubious

honour it was to be a dancer.[3] The women were forbidden from leaving the grounds of the governor's mansion, and, if discovered dallying with other men, severely punished. Like the dancers of the palace, those under the control of the governor were adorned with precious diamonds and gold while performing. But only the 'favourites' acquired any personal wealth. Most of the women lived and ate communally. Meagre rations had them anticipating visits from family who would bring extra provisions. Though admired, even venerated during performance, with the exception of those of royal lineage or those selected as a principal concubine, the dancers were not privileged members of society.

The kings who followed Ang Duong were all patrons of dance to one degree or another, sometimes housing multiple troupes under the palace roof. Khmer kings who had been raised in Siam, including Ang Duong and his sons, brought many Siamese to the court, some of whom were apparently dancers. Mutual cultural exchange between the two countries thus continued.

In 1906 the monarch and the royal dancers embarked on an unprecedented journey. They travelled to France where the dancers performed for the general public. The relationship between the monarchy, classical dance, and Cambodia's past, which had long been used by the court with the aim of uniting the nation, was henceforth projected to the outside world.

In the second quarter of the twentieth century, as the court gradually had fewer resources with which to maintain the tradition, French authorities divided the royal artists. Some were to stay in the palace; others became civil servants. Even though the arrangement was short-lived, this rupture with ancient tradition presaged further disarray in the art of the court. Ultimately, master artist Khun Meak, who had previously been a principal dancer, revived the palace troupe under the patronage of Queen Kossamak Nearyrath.

In the 1940s, after Sihanouk ascended the throne, the dancers' personal circumstances changed. They were free to live outside the confines of the court and to marry, though practise continued in the palace dance halls and their art was still needed as a sacred offering. In addition, the Queen Mother decided to invite men into the royal troupe as dancers of the monkey role. It is not known if

certain types of court dance troupes had always been exclusively female, but at any rate this had been the case for close to a century. It was also at this time that lengthy dance–dramas were significantly shortened to be made compatible with Western theatrical tradition. King Sihanouk entertained Khmer and visiting dignitaries with performances of the royal troupe, and included the dancers in his entourage on diplomatic tours abroad. As part of a presentation to distinguished guests, or on a foreign stage, the dancers would perform an episode or two from a dance–drama along with some newly choreographed 'pure dance' pieces (Plate 31).

With imagery evocative of Cambodia's ancient glory, and with the implied force to influence the fortune of the land and hence her people, classical dance continued to link notions of history, earth, rain, and the heavens with the monarch, but now also with Norodom Sihanouk's particular vision of Cambodia as a modern and independent state. Both inside the country and abroad, Khmer dance of the court tradition was by now well established as a potent symbol of the Cambodian nation.

31. Performance in the Royal Palace for dignitaries while Norodom Sihanouk was Head of State before the 1970 *coup d'etat*. (Courtesy of Missions Etrangères, Paris)

In early 1970 a *coup d'etat* precipitated significant changes in Cambodia's government and its dance traditions. The royal troupe lost its star *Apsara* dancer when Norodom Sihanouk and his family, including Princess Buppha Devi, went into exile. With the overthrow of the monarchy and the establishment of a republican regime, the dancers were no longer officially called upon to mediate between the royalty and the heavens. Yet the notion of the dance as embodying a transcendent essence of the nation remained powerful. Classical dancers still practised each morning in the palace compound, while dancers of school age also joined other budding artists at the University of Fine Arts (the word 'Royal' was dropped from the school's name) for academic classes every afternoon. The dancers continued to perform for audiences of high-ranking officials, tourists, and local residents. They even continued to tour abroad. But the dance was referred to now as *robam boran* (ancient dance), eliminating at least in name any association with royalty. Likewise, official foreign language programmes announced appearances of the 'Classical Khmer Ballet.' Certain lyrics were also reworked to eliminate references to the court. In the dance *Tep Monorom*, for example, originally commissioned by the Queen only a decade or so before, the words 'princes and princesses' were changed to 'men and women'.

When the Khmer Rouge took Phnom Penh in April 1975, all city residents were forced to evacuate their homes and march to the countryside. Along with other arts, dance of the court tradition was banned. The dancers tried to hide their identities as any connection to the royal court or the previous republican government was reason enough to be singled out by the Khmer Rouge for torture or execution. Many dancers and teachers did not survive the regime. Close to four years of unchecked starvation, disease, hard labour, and family separation also broke the bodies and minds of many who did.

Yet the Khmer Rouge failed to break the spirit, or the spirits, of the dance. When Cambodia was liberated from Khmer Rouge rule in early 1979 by the army of neighbouring Vietnam, one of the first impulses, not only of the dancers but also of the common people and national authorities, was to reconstruct classical dance.

Cultural offices in provincial capitals recruited performers. Surviving professional artists as well as novices joined fledgling troupes that performed for crowds of hundreds. They danced with tattered bits of cloth and cardboard crowns as costumes. They danced to music made from whatever instruments they could find. People held many ceremonies, just to rejoice in their new-found freedom, inviting dance and theatre troupes to entertain them.

The capital city of Phnom Penh attracted the majority of professional classical dancers who had survived the regime. 'Swollen and dried by the sun', 'stiff and emaciated', as they recall, it was by dancing—by teaching and performing—that the dancers consciously strove to awaken themselves, their country, and their culture from a collective nightmare. They massaged and coaxed themselves back into shape, performing for local audiences as well as foreign visitors soon after the fall of the Khmer Rouge. Under the guidance of the handful of master artists still alive, perhaps most notably Chea Samy—a dancer presented to the King in the 1920s who was to become a leading practitioner of the female role in court dance—a National Dance Company was created within the Ministry of Culture's Department of Performing Arts, and children were trained in dance technique at the newly re-established School of Fine Arts.[4]

Recognized as a powerful tool of communication in the national and international arenas, classical dance performance was again harnessed for political ends. Like the pre-Khmer Rouge republic before it, the Vietnamese-installed regime imposed changes to lyrics and repertoire. Inserted in the *Apsara* Dance song were words celebrating 'January seventh, Liberation Day', the date when Vietnamese-led forces had ousted the Khmer Rouge from Phnom Penh. New dances honouring the 'friendship' of Cambodia, Laos, and Vietnam, three countries united under the authority of the Vietnamese at that time, were created. Yet older dances were performed as well. Troupes associated with the School of Fine Arts and the Department of Performing Arts toured Cambodia and abroad during the 1980s. Parades marking national holidays, as well as television programmes, featured dancers as they had before the war (Colour Plate 13).

Meanwhile, in refugee camps on the Thai–Cambodian border, where hundreds of thousands of Cambodians lived between 1980 and 1993, dance maintained a high profile. These civilian camps, which were associated with military and political factions allied against the Vietnamese-installed regime in Phnom Penh, each boasted one or more performance troupes (Colour Plate 14). The few court dancers resident in the camps, and even sometimes people with little experience but a deep attachment to the art, opened training centres in bamboo and thatch enclosures. Princess Buppha Devi, living in exile in France, visited the border frequently over the years, lending her expertise to the training of new dancers. She taught in France as well. Indeed, wherever a sizeable number of Cambodian refugees had resettled, whether in Europe, North America, Australia or elsewhere, dance troupes were created. Khmer classical dance has played a central role in maintaining cultural proximity for those people who found themselves geographically distanced from their homeland.

It was not until 1991, with the return of the royalty to Cambodia, that the dancers' link to the monarchy—and the gods—was again officially recognized. Norodom Sihanouk returned after the signing of United Nations-sponsored peace accords aimed at ending more than ten years of civil war between several political and military factions. He was named King again in 1993. His daughter, the dancer Buppha Devi, returned to Cambodia with him, and became a senior adviser to the dancers, as her grandmother had been before her. In early 1999 she was named Minister of Culture and Fine Arts.

Training

Girls and boys embark at the age of eight or nine on the long road to becoming a professional classical dancer. They must learn to evoke meaning through a combination of hand gesture, body posture, and movement, inner understanding of the role and facial expression. Teachers say it takes at least twelve years to be an accomplished dancer—six to master the steps, and another six to understand the spiritual and emotional aspects of the dance, as well

as to perfect the art of performance, the art of communicating atmosphere and story-line.

The articulation and expression of a dancer's hands are highly nuanced. Yet, meaning comes from the totality of the movement and positioning of every part of the body, combined with the music, costume, and sung poetry. Some postures and movements are symbolic; others more realistic, meant to evoke human emotions such as fear, love, anger, and joy. Still others are merely connective, leading the transition from one ephemeral pose to another. Certain hand gestures can have multiple interpretations, depending on how they are combined with other elements of the dance (Plate 32). In classical dance, monkeys cry, princes fly, and goddesses say farewell through combinations of posture, movement, melody, and lyrics.

Training now takes place at the dance division of the Royal University of Fine Arts. Students are selected according to strict criteria: teachers scrutinize muscle development, flexibility, sense

32. Some of the core hand gestures in court dance.
Each can take on various meanings in the context
of performance. (Janet Essley)

of rhythm and balance, and facial structure. New students are type-cast from the start. Girls with a smaller build and rounder faces will study the female roles; those with larger frames and longer faces will play the male and ogre roles. The boys will train to be *lakhon khol* ogres or classical or *khol* monkeys. Practise is rigorous. Discipline is stern. Students go through a strenuous exercise routine to foster the hyperextension and flexibility so central to the dance aesthetic. They also perform a series of thousands of basic postures and movements called *chha banchos* or *kbach baat* over and over again, every day (Colour Plate 15). The series is divided into two cadences, one relatively slow during which dancers execute sustained symmetrical poses and the other faster, when they move across the floor. Only after mastering this sequence, which takes about an hour to complete, may the students learn actual dances and dance–dramas. But even then they must continue daily repetition of the basic movements, the core vocabulary from which Khmer dances are created (Plates 33 and 34).

Students learn through imitation as their teachers dance before them, and by physical manipulation. To ensure the shoulders are down and back, the teacher presses her thumbs just under the dancer's shoulder blades (Plate 35). To correct the placement of a foot lifted off the ground, she will touch (or whack!) the dancer's foot with a rattan stick. The student watches and follows intently. Her (or his) silent, trusting, and active integration of knowledge and skills is one sign of respect for the dance teacher. Another is the weekly presentation of incense. In return for the incense, the teachers ask the spirits of the dance to watch over their students and help them learn quickly.

The *sampeah kru* ceremony honours the sacred nature of the teacher–student relationship. Before every performance and at special occasions throughout the year—when learning a new role, for example—dancers recite prayers as they present lit incense and other offerings to the spirits of the dance, the spirits of deceased dance masters, and to their teachers as part of this ceremony. They give thanks for all they have been privileged to learn, and ask that their teachers stay healthy and strong. They also ask for guidance as they strive to understand and refine a precious part of their cultural

33. Practice costumes consist of traditional pantaloons
and tight-fitting, short-sleeved shirts. (Serey
Bandol, Site 2 Khmer Displaced Persons Camp,
1990; Courtesy of Association Phare)

heritage so that some day they, too, may pass it on to another gen-
eration.

The centre-piece of a collective *sampeah kru* ceremony, which
many from the arts community often attend, is the low table upon
which dance crowns, masks, and accoutrements such as a bow and
an axe are displayed. Plates of food stretch out along the floor in two
long rows before the table. Carved banana-trunk offerings topped

34. Professional dancers in the Ministry of Culture's Department of Performing Arts continue daily repetition of the fundamentals of their art, 1992. (Toni Samantha Phim)

with candles, flowers, and incense stand at the head of the rows. Offerings are also placed before the *sampho* in the *pin peat* ensemble.

A master of ceremonies, seated between the rows of offerings, invokes the spirits of the dance along with the gods Shiva, Vishnu, and Indra and other divine beings (Colour Plate 16). Instructing the musicians, he calls out the name of one sacred tune after another, as the dancers sit reverently, palms together in a position of prayer.

At the proper moment, senior dance masters carry the plates of offerings to the dancers. Then, rising slowly to the accompaniment of a ritual melody, the dancers salute the spirits by lifting the offer-

35. Chea Samy, a great master of the female role in court dance until her death in 1994, moulds a young student into position, 1993. (Toni Samantha Phim)

ings to each of the cardinal directions. Later in the ceremony, the dancers perform excerpts from the series of basic postures and movements specific to their character role.

The ogres, considered to possess the greatest concentration of power, perform first, wielding staffs and executing expansive and deliberate gestures. Those who specialize in male and female roles perform next. Beginning and ending with a stylized posture of prayer and respect (Colour Plate 17), they dance in unison, the stances and movements of the male characters being somewhat wider and higher than those of the female characters. The monkeys are the last to perform, doing somersaults and picking fleas.

Teachers close the ceremony by tying cotton threads doused in lustral water around the wrists of their students. While performing this gesture, meant to secure the vital spirits or souls of the dancers in their bodies, the teachers offer blessings, advice, and admonitions to those entrusted with carrying on their long tradition. Creating a sense of historical and spiritual continuity, the *sampeah*

kru ceremony enhances the potent connection between yesterday, today, and tomorrow for the dancers.

Dancers in a village in Kandal Province, independent of the court or central government institutions, perform classical dances for the changing of the *tevoda* (deities) every New Year and in honour of the spirits of the deceased during the annual Celebration of the Dead. Hundreds of villagers gather in the local temple compound to join in ceremonial prayers and performances. They begin with a *sampeah kru* ceremony, held in the monks' dining hall, in which local ancestral spirits are invoked along with spirits of the dance.

The offerings are much less elaborate than those prepared for a *sampeah kru* ceremony in the capital. The masks and dance accoutrements are tattered and fragile. Accompanied by the local *pin peat* ensemble, the invocations and dancing proceed, punctuated by voices and movements of mediums in trance. One, seated, begins to move her arms, hands, and torso to an internal rhythm. Another is crying, then shaking. Still another executes classical dance movements while standing in place as one more, believed to be possessed by the spirit of an ogre, prances through the crowd, legs lifted in a high gait, elbows bent and raised shoulder height. After this morning ceremony, the dancers perform before the statue of the Buddha, in the temple sanctuary, a practice deemed unorthodox by those in the royal troupe. Later that evening, they perform short dance pieces and a lengthy dance–drama back in the monks' dining hall.

These are remarkable occasions where what can be seen as the most popular of Cambodia's performing arts—possession—literally melds with the nation's most sophisticated and élite form of cultural expression—classical dance. The continuum from the people to the monarchy to the gods is realized through performance, as the spirits of the dance are asked to protect not only the artists but the community as a whole.

A Royal Ritual

Cambodian New Year is celebrated in mid-April, at the height of the hot season, but not long before the first clouds of the rainy season will appear. On this occasion, a connection between the

land and the heavens is reinforced at the national level. Classical dancers present offerings and prayers to the deities on behalf of the monarchy, and thus on behalf of the nation, in a royal ceremony held at the palace or at Vat Phnom, the sacred site of the capital city's foundation. As part of this rite, dancers perform mythical tales in which the women most often represent *tevoda*. Legend has it that at the New Year, new *tevoda* come to watch over Cambodia, exchanging places with those from the year past. One way in which the people of Cambodia ask them for blessings is through performance.

In anticipation of this royal ceremony, plates of food, similar to those in a *sampeah kru* rite, are set out in two rows on a long table. Musicians dress in white high-collared jackets and *kben*. Along with the singers they sit facing the area delineated for the sacred dance at the foot of the table. The dancers walk out in full performance dress and sit in rows according to the character they are portraying: female and male *tevoda*, and ogres. As with the *sampeah kru*, a master of ceremonies calls forth a host of divinities. After the dancers have presented offerings to the cardinal directions, and the ogres have performed their own series of basic movements, the tale begins.

Noble male and elegant female *tevoda* are enjoying each other's company. They dance in lines as the orchestra plays and the chorus sings. The male deities pair off with their female counterparts. Their approach evokes a subtle reaction on the part of the females, who, with an understated pivot of the head away from their companion's gaze, raise their left hands to one cheek in a gesture of feigned bashfulness. Their hesitancy is short-lived as the couples stroll off together, one female preceding one male, arms, hands, and legs flowing in harmony.

Immediately upon the exit of the *tevoda*, the ogre Ream Eyso enters in a fury (Plate 36). Showing off his magic axe, he prances with bold, wide gestures, aiming to take possession of an even more powerful attribute—a jewelled ball just given to Moni Mekhala, goddess of the seas, by their teacher the hermit.

Ream Eyso searches for Moni Mekhala, and finds her playing with her friends, the *tevoda*. He stalks her and threatens the deities

36. The ogre Ream Eyso during a royal ceremony held on the occasion of the Cambodian New Year at Vat Phnom in Phnom Penh, 1969. (B. Dupaigne; Collection Musée de l'Homme, Paris)

who form a protective shield before the goddess. Hands cupped, each *tevoda* quivers in fear. The ogre pushes through the crowd. Ream Eyso and Moni Mekhala are finally face to face.

In temperament and gesture, the two present opposite extremes. The goddess seems to float through space with narrow steps. Ream Eyso struts in confidence. Each time he reaches for the ball, forming a claw with his hand, Moni Mekhala, unfazed, moves effortlessly out of his path.

In desperation, Ream Eyso flings his spangled axe at her, barely missing the goddess. Moni Mekhala then tosses her ball into the air, creating a bolt of lightning that blinds the ogre. He collapses, and Moni Mekhala glides away. Only seconds later he realizes what has happened. He has missed his chance. In frustration and anger, he wipes his prominent brow and retreats into the clouds.

In this tale lies the fabled provenance of thunder and lightning. Ream Eyso's axe crashes through the air and Moni Mekhala's sparkling ball lights up the heavens. Together they bring rain, inaugurating another agricultural season and cycle of life. After the conclusion of the ceremony, people await the darkening of the clouds, and the first rumbles from the sky. They know then that Ream Eyso and Moni Mekhala are engaging in their eternally renewed battle, and that the rice fields will be ready for sowing before long.

1. Norodom Sihanouk became King in 1941. In the 1950s he relinquished his throne to become Head of State of Cambodia, and took the title of Prince. His father, Norodom Suramarit, was then crowned King. Sihanouk was recoronated in 1993 and remains King to this day.

2. Costuming may change slightly from dance to dance, or from one character to another of the same type in a given drama. Male and female characters wear several styles of head-dress, while monkeys and ogres wear masks distinguished by colour and by the shape of the attached crown.

3. Tauch Chhuong, *Battambang Samay Lok Mchas* [Battambang in the Era of Lord Governor], Battambang, Society of Researchers, 1974; 2nd edition, Phnom Penh, Cedoreck, 1994.

4. This school was in fact a reconstituted University of Fine Arts which had been closed along with all other schools under the Khmer Rouge. It was not until 1989 that university-level classes were taught there once again. However, the dance division, though part of the university, incorporates only primary through secondary levels.

4
All-male Dance–Drama

In the closing decades of the nineteenth century, King Norodom, great-grandfather of Norodom Sihanouk, introduced or rehabilitated a national festival called *Tang Tok*.[1] This grand cultural exhibition which projected a vision of diverse traditions united under royal patronage was to be a part of Cambodia's modern nation-building strategy for decades to come. Held on the occasion of the monarch's birthday, the celebration allowed the public to enter the palace compound to partake of displays, games, and performances. Members of the royal family as well as ordinary citizens were offered the chance to admire crafts and produce brought in from Cambodia's provinces, and to be entertained by a variety of theatrical offerings. One of these was *lakhon khol*, an all-male masked dance–drama representing sequences from the *Reamker*. Though the *lakhon khol* tradition is presumably much older, nineteenth-century accounts provide the earliest definitive documentation of the dance genre as it is known today.

Composed of dance, mimed gesture, and chanted narration, all accompanied by a *pin peat* ensemble, the formal and thematic roots of *lakhon khol* are to be found in the *Reamker* of the classical dance tradition. Yet one intriguing aspect of *khol* is in fact its many differences from the classical tradition—and its relative separation from the court. The all-male troupe which performed at Norodom's *Tang Tok* came from a village across the Mekong River to play only periodically at the palace. The dancers are the spiritual, if not the actual successors of male dancers reputed to have been maintained at the court during the reign of Ang Duong. After Ang Duong's death, the male troupe is said to have been dissolved, only to be reconstituted later under the patronage of Norodom, but in a village context, across the river from Phnom Penh. In the beginning

of the twentieth century, one observer of court dance noted the existence of some sixty male dancers of the *Reamker* across the country who were periodically called upon to perform at the palace.[2]

In *lakhon khol* performance at the palace around the turn of the century, Reab and his fellow ogres wore fanged masks similar to those of classical tradition. Monkeys of high rank donned the masks of the court dance, while those representing ordinary soldiers in Preah Ream's army appeared in more realistic and unadorned monkey masks. Preah Ream and his brother Preah Leak were masked in green and pinkish-white respectively. Seda and her attendants, played by men of petite stature and delicate features, appeared with faces painted in thick white powder. Many of the masks, golden head-dresses, and richly layered costumes were previously used by or on loan from the court dance troupe.

The all-male dance troupe of the late-nineteenth-century governor of Battambang Province, mentioned in Chapter 3, performed only episodes from the *Reamker*, while his female troupe had a broader repertoire. As opposed to the women who remained cloistered in the governor's compound, the male dancers, numbering more than 100, performed as requested at individual temples and under official patronage. One such occasion was the governor-instituted annual celebration, akin to the *Tang Tŏk* ceremony in Phnom Penh, in which tribute was paid to the Siamese king, as Battambang was at that time under Siamese rule.

Descriptions of one performance by this troupe are particularly striking. At the Buddhist ordination of the governor's son, dancers depicting Preah Ream's troops, in full costume and riding on horseback, confronted others dressed as Reab's warriors, riding buffaloes, before the temple. Each brigade was accompanied by its own *pin peat* ensemble. After victory, Preah Ream and his soldiers escorted the future monk into the temple.[3] In traditional ordination ceremonies, future monks often arrive at the temple clad in regalia and on horseback. This is a well-known allusion to the life of the Buddha who was a young prince before becoming a monk. In the Battambang governor's son's ceremony, the induction into the Buddhist order was preceded instead by a spectacular evocation of the *Reamker*, a legend of Brahmanic origin.

The legacy of the governor's *lakhon khol* troupe continued with at least one other group in Battambang throughout most of the twentieth century, until political unrest and war brought about its demise.

The Svay Andet Troupe

In the village of Svay Andet, Kandal Province, across the Mekong River from Phnom Penh, a renowned *lakhon khol* company—the descendant of those that played at *Tang Tok* festivals for decades—remains active. It was in fact the skill of Svay Andet's 'monkeys' which inspired Kossamak Nearyrath to introduce male dancers into the court troupe. She recruited boys from the *khol* troupe she had seen at a 1940s *Tang Tok* festival to dance the monkey role inside the palace. But the Svay Andet troupe, the only traditional company to have survived the war, has long been renowned less for its palace associations than for its traditional New Year's celebration during which dancers enact numerous sequences from the *Reamker* over the course of seven nights.

Various spiritual trajectories mingle and fuse in the multilayered event involving *lakhon khol* held at New Year's time. Through performance, villagers seek to propitiate ancestral spirits and to ensure divine benevolence for the village as a whole. The performance almost always includes the Battle of Kumbhakar which concludes with the release of heavenly waters. Kumbhakar, brother of the ogre king Reab, has stretched his enlarged body across a river, damming its waters and depriving Preah Ream's men downstream of necessary sustenance. The monkey chief Hanuman and his monkey ally Angkut counter this ruse. Angkut transforms himself into a floating dead dog; Hanuman becomes a crow feeding on the corpse. Kumbhakar fails repeatedly to drive off the two animals, and, unable to bear the stench, leaps up in anger to strike them, releasing the waters.

The New Year's *lakhon khol* festival in Svay Andet has a profoundly magical purpose. The representation is meant literally as a performative act. The performance of the release of water in the *Reamker* is meant to realize the release of water in Cambodia itself,

the arrival of monsoon rains. In this grandiose annual theatrical production, earthly cycles are directly identified with the divine legend; villagers directly identify with the *Reamker*. The fact that the *khol* version of the *Reamker* differs significantly from the classical text taught in schools, and from the one recited in *sbaek thom* performance, can be attributed, at least in part, to the art's specific magico-therapeutic function. The epic tale has undoubtedly evolved thematically and structurally in the rural ritual context, where strict adherence to tradition is constantly tempered by improvisation responding to changing social conditions and needs.

The magic role of the Svay Andet company can in fact extend to other occasions. Older dancers recall, for example, a seven-night-long performance (some recall it lasting fourteen nights) staged in the pre-war period to combat a cholera epidemic, which was itself attributed to negligence of the performance tradition. In more recent times, episodes of the tale have been performed to ask for peace. The perpetuation of tradition is perceived as carrying the possibility of combating communal ills and re-establishing natural and social order.

Indeed, *lakhon khol* incorporates active participation by many members of the community. The performers are villagers too, who work as farmers, teachers, and so on, throughout the year. Performances, including ceremonial invocations, are attended by hundreds from Svay Andet as well as from neighbouring villages. During the performance, held now exclusively at night, spectators comment aloud upon the story and the characters. Children are involved in the performance from an early age. At times enthralled with the action, they are at other moments found scurrying across the performance space, unintimidated by the choreographed confrontations going on around them.

Like other traditions, *lakhon khol* was threatened with permanent disappearance by the Khmer Rouge regime. Performances were banned. Artists were subjected to extreme physical and emotional hardship. In addition, the manuscript text of the *khol Reamker* which had served as the only written support for the Svay Andet troupe for decades, if not centuries, disappeared from the local temple treasury where it had always been stored. Surviving dancers

regrouped in the 1980s and, with the support of the Ministry of Culture's Department of Performing Arts, rekindled the Svay Andet tradition. However, the troupe is now greatly reduced in number; performances never last more than three consecutive nights. While the Svay Andet New Year's celebration remains intact in the memory of many Cambodians, the death of one of its troupe leaders (Colour Plate 18), extreme material penury, and the onslaught of modernity with its cheap videos and mass tourism have greatly endangered the *lakhon khol* tradition as a meaningful popular ritual.

Before the first night of the Svay Andet New Year's performance, troupe members and other villagers celebrate an extremely elaborate version of the *sampeah kru* ritual. As with any *sampeah kru* ceremony preceding dramatic performance, homage is paid to the Buddha and the Brahmanic gods, and to the ancestral teachers and spirits of the arts. The Svay Andet villagers and *lakhon khol* players also invoke divinities specific to the *Reamker* tradition as it has been integrated into the village through performance.

The ceremony requires days of preparation. Offerings of food, candles, and incense are placed in small sanctuaries or altars situated on the temple grounds proper or on the adjoining terrain reserved for performance, and which are believed to harbour individual spirits associated with the dance–drama (Colour Plate 19). The performance pavilion, a wooden rectangular structure enclosed only at one end and with wooden railings on either side, is prepared for the ceremony as for a performance. Mats are laid on the ground within the pavilion. Participants will sit at the open end of the space, next to the *pin peat* orchestra and narrators or ritual officiants. Spectators will sit further behind, and also crowd around the pavilion's sides. At the closed end of the pavilion, in front of a wooden or cloth divider marking the back of the stage, masks and head-dresses are arranged on an altar. Though there used to be a slightly raised stage, since the war of the 1970s dancers perform on ground level. Offerings are arranged in two rows running the length of the performance space.

The *sampeah kru* ceremony proper, held after sunset, is in fact a performance. While initial Buddhist prayers are solemn, the atmosphere soon becomes rapidly charged, even raucous, with drums

and screams punctuating the subsequent musical and chanted invocations. Lengthy reference is made to the ancestral masters and protective divinities of *sbaek thom*, as if the shadow theatre interpretation of the *Reamker* were itself a revered ancestor of *khol*.

The remarkable specificity of the *lakhon khol sampeah kru*—and in many ways of *lakhon khol* itself—is the central role played by village mediums. Those divinities worshipped on sanctuary altars across the temple and performance grounds come to possess the bodies of older dance masters or other village mediums on stage. The *lakhon khol sampeah kru* is, in some senses, a collective, choreographed trance. Accompanied by the *pin peat* orchestra and intoned recitations, the mediums burst onto stage from behind the rear divider or from the audience. They dance and engage in dialogue with each other and with the spectators, demanding the strict respect of tradition. They lament, for example, the reduced duration of the performance, and demand that at least the three-day version be maintained. They order villagers to reject popular culture emanating from Phnom Penh which threatens to bring on disaster. Only adherence to truly traditional practices, they say in menacing tones, will ensure the well-being of the community. Some mediums collapse dramatically as they come out of possession, to revive minutes later; others leave the pavilion still in trance. Their performance is interspersed with dance sequences performed by the young dancers and their teachers (Colour Plate 20). The mediums bless the dancers and spectators by sprinkling the crowd with lustral water.

Sometime prior to the performance of the featured story, a complementary ceremony is held inside the central temple sanctuary. Dancers present their masks and head-dresses to the Buddha while dancing before his statue.

Each night's performance opens with a series of *pin peat* melodies and the representation of each character type through dance. The mediums also participate in this opening by dancing and interacting with the troupe and the spectators on and off stage. Re-enactment of the epic tale can be periodically interrupted by one or more of the mediums who take to the stage to comment upon the action or, again, to demand strict conformity with tradition.

With the mediums as an integral part of the troupe and of the performance, Svay Andet's *lakhon khol* demonstrates the continuum between possession and dramatic performance which is obscured in more elaborate or 'modern' theatre and dance forms. The mediums' principal mode of expression is dance, even though, relative to trained dancers, they may move awkwardly. And, like mediums, the dancers incarnate other-worldly characters.

Lakhon khol technique is transmitted through direct apprentice-ship in the village. Three types of masters teach four types of roles: ogres, monkeys, and princes and princesses. Though training is rigorous, requiring intense mental and physical concentration, it is significantly less formalized than that offered dancers in the capital. The ritual relationship between master and disciple, who are often members of the same family, is, however, equally important in the village context.

Fundamentally nurtured by the Buddhist temple, this popular dance troupe maintains strong symbolic associations to the court along with some more practical ties to central cultural authorities. Older masters of the Svay Andet troupe inculcate in their young disciples the importance of the palace association. They recall their own palace performances, and claim royal origins for their tradi-tion. Like the seven-day performance or the 'complete' manuscript text, the association has been lost in practice but not in memory. Much of the jewellery and many of the masks and costumes, kept at the palace until the 1970s, are now stored at the Department of Performing Arts in Phnom Penh, and borrowed for performance. As was the case a century ago, many of these accoutrements origin-ally belonged to the classical troupe. Some are inferior copies. Evolution in *khol* presentation even seems to have in some ways followed the classical example. Today's Svay Andet *khol* princes, for example, no longer wear masks like their nineteenth-century pre-decessors, but are instead made-up with cosmetics like their clas-sical counterparts. The Department of Performing Arts periodically invites the Svay Andet troupe to perform in festivals in the capital or in other provinces.

Although aspects of performance story-line, costuming, music, and even movement are similar to those of the royal ensemble,

lakhon khol is in many ways its reverse image. The most obvious contrast is the use of an all-male cast in *khol*. Another contrast not unrelated to this gender difference is that while classical dance focuses predominantly on the interaction and adventures of the cultivated and highly restrained princes and princesses, *lakhon khol* emphasizes the actions of the decidedly masculine and aggressive ogres and monkeys.

As in each dance genre discussed thus far, the drama in *lakhon khol* is propelled by music, recitation, and movement. The dancers alternate between miming the action as it is recounted, and dancing to musical interludes, a mixture that recalls *sbaek thom*, and to a certain degree classical *Reamker* performance. For all of these performance traditions, each sequence of gestures and postures expressing specific emotions or actions corresponds to a distinct melody. Intoned recitation in *lakhon khol*, which communicates emotions and story-line, is provided by two or three men sitting off to the side next to the orchestra. Their technique, as well as their role in arranging the overall performance, resembles those of the *sbaek thom* narrators. Also as in *sbaek thom*, the narration alternates between different types of poetic prose and verse. Court dance, we have noted, has choral accompaniment rather than intoned recitation. Furthermore, as opposed to the more discreet use of *skor thom* during classical dance performance, these large drums dominate the *lakhon khol* orchestra. They mark rhythmic emphasis in the dance, and signal transitions in musical sequences.

Subtle differences exist between the codified gestural language of classical dance and that of *khol*. Stronger divergence can be noted in overall style of movement. In *lakhon khol*, the giants shift their weight and move their torsos and heads in quick, almost jerky bursts. They appear somewhat stiffer than the giants played by women in classical dance. The manoeuvring of the *lakhon khol* monkeys is a bit more naturalistic than that of the classical dance monkeys. In particular, the *khol* monkeys of lesser rank run on all fours and sit with hunched shoulders, glancing puckishly from side to side.

Difference in performance setting also affects choreography and technique. *Khol* performers enact the story while either sitting on

the railing or dancing on the long mats lining the ground. When seated, an ogre, for example, moves his head, upper body and arms to the recitation provided by a narrator. He periodically lifts his torso and hips away from the rail, then lowers them to resume sitting, for emphasis, all the while with his legs in a turned-out position. Marching and battle scenes transpire away from the rail, on the woven mats.

Professional Performance

Taught at the Royal University of Fine Arts since its establishment in the 1960s, *lakhon khol* has developed somewhat differently in institutional and professional contexts around the country. In the 1980s and 1990s, the Kompong Thom Office of Culture, a provincial branch of the Ministry of Culture, created new *khol* pieces for the theatrical stage. These include a one-hour performance with an original dramatic story-line, animated with characters from the *Reamker*. It is performed by a mixed cast of women and men, with all of the male characters masked, including Preah Ream. Another work, developed in 1999 in collaboration with the Department of Performing Arts, is an extended treatment of the Kumbhakar episode danced only by men, again with Preah Ream and Preah Leak in masks. This piece includes an episode called Battle at Night which was brought to the capital as a discrete dance in the 1980s and further refined. The episode is danced to the music of the *pin peat* orchestra, but no lyrics are recited or sung. A fight between ogres and monkeys erupts after two monkeys discover that a friend has been captured by the ogres (Plate 37). The confrontation happens at night, and becomes somewhat slapstick when the lanterns the monkeys have been holding are knocked out of their hands by the thick long wands manipulated by the ogres. Combatants on each side hit, kick, and nearly stab their allies as they grope in the dark for their enemies. One monkey eventually recovers his lantern, and in the new-found light the monkeys manage to down the ogres with their daggers. The stage lights are dimmed during the comic interlude when the monkeys and the ogres are fighting in the dark. The lights regain their intensity

37. A monkey (*above*) and an ogre engage in battle
in a *lakhon khol* performance. (Janet Essley)

when the lantern is found, thereby adding dramatic force to the
conclusion of the dance.

Unlike Svay Andet's *lakhon khol*, Battle at Night does not present
excerpts from the *Reamker* with specific character portrayal,
though it did when originally choreographed. It is rather a gener-
alized representation of a leitmotiv found in much of the Khmer
dramatic repertoire: good, represented by monkeys who are never-
theless uncouth, has triumphed over evil, the ogres. Professional
artists see this as a metaphor for the enlightenment that Cambodia
needs in the face of the destruction and loss engendered by war.

Included in the repertoire of both the Department of Performing Arts and the University, this version of *lakhon khol*, still all
male, lasts about ten minutes. It is performed in sumptuous costumes of velvet and brocade (Colour Plate 21), often as part of a
review including classical and folk dances.

Since Phnom Penh's *lakhon khol* performers have trained in the
fundamentals of court dance for years, their postures adhere to a

63

strict canon. Yet, they are also given more latitude for improvisation or embellishment than are their classical dance counterparts. As opposed to the more discreet nature of a battle scene in the court *Reamker*, Battle at Night is athletic and acrobatic as the ogres and monkeys use each other's weight and climb upon each other's thighs and shoulders.

One of the current teachers of *lakhon khol* at the Royal University of Fine Arts, Yith Sarin, was among the first 'monkeys' to be spotted during *Tang Tok*, and left the Svay Andet troupe to join the royal dancers more than half a century ago (Plate 38). Frequently returning to his home village to work with young dancers, he continues to further mutual exchange between dance traditions.

38. Yith Sarin training University of Fine Arts students, 1991. (James Wasserman)

1. It is possible that something similar to *Tang Tok* has existed since Angkorian times. See Bernard-Philippe Groslier, *Inscriptions du Bayon, Mémoires Archéologiques 3*, Paris, Ecole Française d'Extrême-Orient, 1973, pp. 132–3 and 160.

2. Georges Groslier, *Danseuses Cambodgiennes*, Paris, Augustin Challamel, 1913, p. 67, n. 1.

3. Tauch Chhuong, *Battambang Samay Lok Mchas* [Battambang in the Era of Lord Governor], Battambang, Association of Researchers, 1974; second edition Phnom Penh, Cedoreck, 1994, pp. 127–8.

5
Ceremonial and Theatrical Folk Dance

THIS chapter treats dance which is largely distinct from court arts in terms of story-line, costuming, and performance setting. Two subgroups are distinguished within this 'folk' genre. The first, Ceremonial Folk Dance, includes dances still performed as part of popular ritual celebrations today. The second, Theatrical Folk Dance, covers urban interpretations and adaptations of these same ritual performances, and of daily activities in the countryside, as choreographed for the stage by professional dancers.

Ceremonial Folk Dance

Khmer New Year's celebrations in mid-April boast an array of ritual performances related to seasonal change. Two of these have been discussed in previous chapters: an offering and prayer ceremony featuring royal dancers and an all-male masked dance–drama. Here, we will briefly discuss two other village-based examples: *Trot*, and the Wild Buffalo Horn Dance. Though their exact origins, along with their ritual functions, are veiled in layers of myth and hearsay, both of these dances are thought by scholars to be derived from ancient ritual associated with annual renewal. Likewise, performers understand and present the dances as remnants of an ancient past. Some similarities between *Trot* and the Wild Buffalo Horn Dance in both form and function might suggest that either the different traditions have converged, or one form has differentiated over time. Whatever their kinship, they are performed today as distinct dance-rituals associated with distinct regions.

Trot is an itinerant dance representing a deer hunt. It is generally seen only in the northwestern province of Siem Reap and neighbouring Battambang, as well as in Thailand's Surin Province where

ethnic Khmer still uphold ancestral tradition. *Trot* has also been documented in other more southerly regions of Cambodia where the court is known to have resided in the post-Angkorian period. This particular localization of the tradition lends support to theories and legends which posit that today's primarily popular ritual was once associated in one way or another with the monarchy. It is possible that *Trot* troupes were once composed of villagers, even members of an ethnic minority, who paid some sort of annual tribute to the king through dance. Indeed, after having performed in numerous villages, *Trot* troupes in Siem Reap generally end their annual peregrination at Angkor Vat. In this ancient temple dedicated to the memory of a twelfth-century king associated with the Brahmanic god Vishnu, they dance before statues of the Buddha, statues themselves still associated with Cambodia's deceased monarchs.[1]

As with so many of the arts and religious rites of Cambodia, the symbolism of *Trot* has long been adapted to reflect a Buddhist sensibility even while it maintains connections to older ancestral beliefs. For example, it is widely held that *Trot* performance wards off catastrophe. These beliefs, and the *Trot* tradition, are deeply rooted in ideas regarding regulation of the agrarian cycle. However, *Trot*'s principal goal of ensuring prosperity is attained in practical terms by reinforcing the Buddhist community network. A central component of the dance is the solicitation of offerings for the troupe's local monastery. By presenting money, food, or other goods to the *Trot* troupe, spectators simultaneously support the ritual tradition and the religious community, and gain merit for themselves.

For anywhere from a few days to a couple of weeks, a *Trot* ensemble will wander from house to house, village to village, bringing song and dance to all they encounter. Before setting out, the performers typically build a spirit house inside which they place offerings. Through prayer in front of this structure, they ask the local ancestral spirits for permission to perform, and for protection along the way. Prayers may also be addressed to Preah Pisnukar, legendary architect of Angkor Vat and patron of the arts, as well as to the Buddhist 'Triple Gem' (the Buddha, the Dharma [Buddha's Teachings], and the Sangha [the community of monks]). Many

troupes inaugurate their journey by performing in the local temple before the image of the Buddha.

The composition of a troupe varies from one ensemble to the next, and even from one year to the next. Two or more players hold *kancha*, tall bamboo poles topped with two arcs curved up and joined to the pole at their intersection through a large hollowed seed containing small stones, seeds, or pieces of metal. Held straight up and tapped against the ground, the *kancha* poles, with their rattling seeds, set the rhythmic pattern of the dance. One or two people back up the rhythm with hand-held goblet drums (*skor areak*). Other musicians play the *tro sau* and *tro ou* (fiddles) and the *pey or* or *pey bobos*, a bamboo flute with an attached reed. Several players also sing lyrics both individually and in unison.

Performers with masked or painted faces, who represent people of the forest, demons, or hunters, move with a lively gait to the rhythm of the drums (Plate 39). A deer, and sometimes one or two wild buffaloes, prance here and there. The deer is incarnated by a player either riding a pole with a deer head fashioned in papier mâché or rattan at the front end and a reed tail at the other, or wearing a headpiece designed to resemble a deer head. Or, sometimes, the player of the deer, like those of the wild buffaloes, simply wears horns. The horns can be real, attached to rattan and placed on the dancer's head, or made from paper covering a rattan frame. These performers often wear bells around their waists.

Two other players, whose primary function is dance, wear 20 to 30 centimetre-long fingernails fashioned from rattan. By clicking their nails together, they also reinforce the rhythm of the *kancha* poles. In some troupes still more dancers carry peacock feathers. One or two others who dance while soliciting offerings complete the entourage. These men or women balance a long curved bamboo pole on one hip. A bag hangs from the far end of the pole ready to receive gifts from spectators. As most rural houses in Cambodia are raised on stilts, the long pole reaches up to people as they watch the dance from the balcony above.

Villagers can hear the approach of *Trot* dancers from afar. Bells jingle; *kancha* poles rattle; drums resound. Upon reaching the front gate of a house, the troupe sings a request to enter the yard and

39. *Trot* performed during the New Year, Siem Reap Province, 1931.
(H. Marchal; Collection Musée de l'Homme, Paris)

perform. In greeting the *Trot*, a household sets out customary offerings made to guests and spirits: woven mats, a bowl of lustral water, a tray of betel chew, candles, and incense.

With other instrumentalists, the *kancha* players form a semicircle or line which roughly demarcates the back of the performance space. They slowly rock backward and forward in unison, their movement reiterating the general rhythm of the performance. With a crossbow slung over his shoulder, or sometimes brandishing a rifle, the hunter, often a comic figure, darts left and right, eyes glancing furtively. Ever alert, the deer and buffalo try to evade the hunter. With fingers rolled into fists and elbows bent, arms forward, they mimic the movements of a cautious and sometimes startled animal. When there are two buffaloes, the pair performs a sort of mating dance, similar to the Wild Buffalo Horn Dance. Meanwhile, the performers holding the curved donation poles leave one hand free to trace graceful patterns in the air while moving from place to place in vaguely circular patterns. They, along with the dancers wearing long fingernails and those with peacock feathers, walk and sway to the drum beat, with movements

similar to those of the popular *roam vong* social dance. One hand and then the other is raised to about eye level; then lowered, with elbows kept slightly bent. The fingers are flexed as the wrists twist in toward the body and out again. Traditionally, the deer is killed at the conclusion of the dance. Struck by the hunter's arrow or bullet, the deer dancer falls, abandons his animal accoutrements and leaves the performance space.

A variety of songs, differing from troupe to troupe, makes up the repertoire of *Trot*. Many of the lyrics are improvised. Singers take as their cues the circumstances of the particular performance. Beseeching onlookers for gifts, they may sing about the grandeur of a household or the lack of specific items at the temple for which they are raising funds. Some documented songs make reference to the arrival of the rains or the concomitant buffalo mating season.

The audience offers money or other gifts, placing them in the bag bobbing from the pole. Before taking their leave and proceeding to the next house, the performers sing a song to bless their benefactors. The *achar*, a lay ritual specialist who often leads the *Trot* procession, sprinkles members of the household with lustral water. Spectators can return the blessing by sprinkling water on the troupe members. A meal is sometimes offered to the troupe in final recompense for the performance. Money and other goods are generally handed over to the temple upon return, at which time the monks perform chants, and bless the troupe.

There are many different explanations of the origin or meaning of *Trot*. Elders in one Siem Reap village today tell a story similar to ones documented by researchers in the 1940s: Once upon a time, there lived a poor hunter named Pon who built a three-storey spirit house at a fork in a forest path. Every morning he made an offering of rice there and prayed to the spirits to help him find an animal he could shoot for dinner. And each day he was successful. Eventually the god Indra saw that Pon had committed great sin by killing so many animals. He sent a *tevoda* to earth disguised as a golden deer to dash across Pon's path. Pon pursued and killed the deer. Pon and his wife decided to offer the unusual bounty to the king, who subsequently invited the couple to live in the palace and cease hunting. Within a week of moving into the palace, Pon and his wife

died. In good Buddhist faith, their deaths were understood as the inevitable result of their accumulated sin. A year later, at the New Year, the king ordered a re-enactment of the story in memory of the couple and the deer. And this is how the *Trot* came to be.

Another popular legend places the origin of the dance as an episode in the life of the Buddha: Before he had attained enlightenment, the Buddha was walking one day along a forest path when a spirit metamorphosed into a deer in order to block his passage. Brahma and Indra disguised themselves as dark-faced demons and descended to earth to kill the deer. Once the path was cleared, these divinities, along with celestial dancers, musicians, and revellers, accompanied the Buddha as he continued on his way.

In both of these legends, the deer signifies danger. Certainly, through *Trot* performance, the animal figures the eruption of the untamed into the village context. This is a threat to traditional order based on the fundamental opposition between the safe, civilized village and the unsafe, wild forest. However, the deer's dangerous nature may well exceed the undomesticated aspects of an animal which, after all, is not ferocious. Arriving at the New Year, the deer represents danger potentially more catastrophic than that which any wild animal could bring: the danger of drought.

The pursuit of the deer, particularly the golden deer, is a theme common to many Asian cultures. The golden-furred animal is frequently associated with the sun, its slaughter with the end of drought. Human mastery of natural cycles figured by the deer hunt is moreover associated with the king. That is, the royal charge of ensuring prosperity across the land is frequently represented through the pursuit and slaughter of the evasive and prized animal. The slaying of the deer which may represent a symbolic slaying of the king (who will be reanimated with renewed force) engenders the return of order. The king rewards the hunter, the Buddha continues on his path to enlightenment. Indeed, in another version of the second tale cited above, after the slaughter of the deer, the Buddha continues on his path *in the rain*.[2] The Buddhist symbolism is but a thin veneer on an archaic ritual. In many cultures, the passage from one year to the next is marked by a brief disruption of social order, a disruption that creates the conditions for a renewal

of the very order it disturbs. The word *Trot* is in fact thought to be the Sanskrit *truṭi*, signifying 'separation', 'break', even 'destruction'.

These days provincial authorities and even monasteries request performances on various other occasions, such as ceremonies marking the beginning and the end of the monks' rainy season retreat, or the cremation of religious dignitaries. In Siem Reap Province, *Trot* troupes perform frequently for tourist groups.

Another version of this dance-ritual, *Trot Neang Meov*, which serves explicitly to ask for rain, is performed not only during the New Year festival but also somewhat later in the year, when upland rice is planted. The same basic characters compose this kind of *Trot* performance, but the deer is replaced by *Neang Meov*, a female cat whose proper name *Meov* is an onomatopoeia of her cry. Two performers, often wearing masks with distorted features similar to those worn by the demons or hunters discussed earlier, carry the cat in a rattan cage suspended between them on a pole balanced on their shoulders. As the troupe moves from house to house, people approach and pour water over the cat, an act believed to bring forth the rains needed for the new crop. Some players may carry woven fish traps and others round woven baskets. They mime gathering fish and tossing them in the baskets as the singers joke about having caught tiny or huge fish depending on the amount of money presented by the audience. The fishing mime, which can also appear in regular *Trot* performance, replaces the solicitation of offerings with long bamboo poles.

The Wild Buffalo Horn Dance may also be performed at New Year's as a way of appealing for rain and prosperity. This ritual dance, which portrays two buffaloes mating, is largely associated with the Peur ethnic group, and with Battambang, Pursat, Kompong Chhnang and Kompong Speu, provinces in which the Peur have lived. It is also performed in other regions at rites celebrated around the same time of year in homage to ancestral spirits, and can be integrated into possession ceremonies.

Descriptions of the dance over the course of the twentieth century present variations on a basic scenario. Two dancers wearing buffalo heads or horned headpieces made of papier mâché or rattan, sometimes incorporating real horns (Plate 40), engage in mock

combat or mating frolics. Two other dancers don peacock feather headdresses and strut about. Traditionally associated with the sun, the peacocks also symbolize the mating ritual. The third dancing role tends to be that of a man (or men) on horseback or simply a horse, with the dancer riding a hobby-horse or wearing a horse headpiece. This is an aggressive character, who serves in general to disrupt the other dancers as well as the spectators. In some cases, hunters replace the horseman, and the dance ends violently as in *Trot*. None the less, the Wild Buffalo Horn Dance basically represents the buffalo rutting season which accompanies the return of the rains each year.

The orchestra generally consists of a *ploy*, a wind instrument made of a dried gourd with bamboo pipes, as well as drums and *kancha* poles.

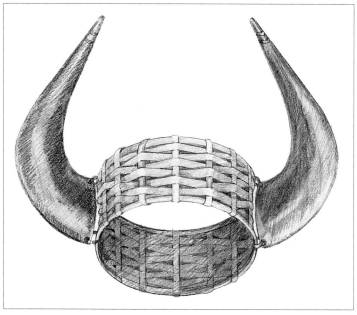

40. Head-dress made from real buffalo horns worn in the Wild Buffalo Horn Dance. (Peg Connor Shapiro)

72

Theatrical Folk Dance

In the 1960s, a 'folk traditions' section was established at Cambodia's Royal University of Fine Arts. Charged with the dual missions of cultural preservation and creation, artists in this newly created dance field spent months in various regions of Cambodia's countryside, gathering information and inspiration for dances they would later develop for stage performance. According to dancers of that time, they believed that if they could refine and beautify some local performance traditions, they might help to stimulate interest in these arts throughout Cambodia, thereby impeding the loss of the country's artistic heritage. The Ministry of Education, which oversaw the Royal University of Fine Arts at that time, was joined in this effort by Queen Kossamak Nearyrath who offered both personal and palace funds to a mission which, she told the artists, she hoped would raise the value of all aspects of Cambodian art and culture in the eyes of all Cambodians.

Teachers, many of whom were not trained dancers but rather professional actors, travelled to various provinces to observe and learn from local ritual specialists, dancers, and musicians. When they heard of dances that were performed only rarely, such as the Wild Buffalo Horn Dance, the artists from Phnom Penh interviewed old practitioners, asked for demonstrations, and recorded their observations of rhythm and gesture in notebooks. They tape-recorded musical accompaniment when they had the resources to do so. Eventually, provincial artists were also brought to the Royal University of Fine Arts campus where they conducted master classes.

The repertoire resulting from reworked regional or ethnic rites included dances based on *Trot* and the Wild Buffalo Horn Dance, among others (Colour Plate 22). In the hands of the dance and music teachers and students of the capital city, ritual performances were stylized and refined to fit the aesthetic of the official arts institution, and the constraints of a proscenium stage. Set lyrics replaced extemporizing, while precise choreography superseded spontaneity of movement. The dances inspired by ritual performances were termed 'traditional' (*propeiney*).

In the theatrical version of the Wild Buffalo Horn Dance, slow

rhythm and intense concentrated movement evoke a trance-like atmosphere. Two wild buffalo dancers—with papier mâché head-pieces fashioned after thick animal horns or woven rattan crowns topped with real horns—and one man playing the *ploy* appear, with a singer and a drummer seated behind them. The singer represents a hunter who, in one story connected with the origin of the ritual version of this dance, was ordered by the king to capture a wild buffalo. The drummer is the tiger who, also in the story, came across two buffaloes dancing, and tapped his paws in accompaniment. So taken were they with the beauty of the mating dance, neither the hunter nor the tiger could attack.

On stage the buffaloes and the *ploy* player begin on their knees, prostrating themselves as the singer invokes Preah Pisnukar. The three then circle the performance space and engage in movements while squatting and while standing, the long pipes of the *phloy* cutting waves through the air. Each buffalo, arms forward and crossed at the wrist, flicks his hands downward on the beat. The singer and drummer remain seated throughout. No peacocks or horses, present in the ritual version, are represented.

Beyond these new interpretations of provincial expressive and ritual culture, elements of what had been observed in the countryside, including movement patterns used in rice planting, folk stories, instrumentation, or melodic sequences and costuming were combined in the creation of completely new 'popular' dances (*robam pracheapriy*) to be performed in a theatre. The Good Crops Dance, representing the Tumpuon and other ethnic minority groups in Mondulkiri and Ratanakiri provinces, and the Mouth Organ Dance, representing ethnic Lao in Stung Treng and other provinces, are such creations. In addition, the artists choreographed other 'popular' pieces (the Fishing, Rice Harvesting, and Pestle Dances, for example) meant to evoke the atmosphere of daily life among the ethnic Khmer in the countryside. These processes—both reworking an established form of expression and conceiving and actualizing a new composition—involved a dose of stereotyped imagery of the people they meant to portray. With the intended audience for these dances primarily Cambodian, the professional artists were in a sense creating idealized reflections of Cambodia

and its inhabitants which would be presented back to the people as lessons about their country and their compatriots.

Folk dance students of the Royal University of Fine Arts performed throughout the provinces. Before each dance, a narrator explained the meaning and provenance of the piece. Theatrical folk dances were taught in teacher-training colleges. They were also featured, along with works from the classical repertoire, in films by then Prince Norodom Sihanouk, shown throughout the country as entertainment at various ceremonies and celebrations. The University troupe, in addition, performed these dances at international folk festivals in the 1960s and early 1970s.

Throughout the 1980s, after establishment of the Ministry of Culture's Department of Performing Arts and the reopening of the School of Fine Arts following the defeat of the Khmer Rouge, more folk dances were created. Again, the aim of these dances was both to entertain and educate by presenting staged representations of regional activities (such as cardamom picking among the Peur ethnic group in Pursat Province in the Cardamom Picking Dance) (Colour Plate 23) along with more generic countryside scenes (such as farmers stopping their rice pounding and threshing to partake of sweet palm juice in a piece entitled Rice Threshing). Folk dance performance troupes from both the Department of Performing Arts and the Royal University of Fine Arts continue to tour Cambodia and abroad.

Theatrical folk dance movements share some characteristics with those of classical dance. Arched backs, bent knees, and flexed fingers lend many of the folk dances, even those with lively syncopated rhythms, a feeling of physical groundedness similar to the earth-bound focus of court dance movement. Arms do not reach to the sky; toes are rarely pointed. While professional folk dancers must master the same series of basic movements during their initial training as do classical dancers, they go on to study a separate set of fundamental folk dance rhythms and movement patterns.

One of the most frequently performed University-created folk dances in Cambodia today is the Fishing Dance in which young men and women meet on an outing ostensibly to catch fish. Women glide in from stage right holding bamboo trays used to

scoop fish from the water as the men, carrying fish traps, enter from the opposite side of the stage to join them. First in male/female pairs, and then in segregated lines and circles, they mirror the gestures of fisherfolk at work.

Costuming for this kind of folk dance is kept simple. The women wear *kben* held up by silver belts. Over their cotton blouses they wrap scarves—either the traditional checkered scarf (*kroma*) or one of a plain colour. The men sport *kroma* around their heads. Loose pants reach to mid-calf while their short-sleeved cotton shirts extend just below the waist. They use a scarf, ends hanging down to the side, in lieu of a belt.

The dancers mime anticipation and excitement with exaggerated expressions as they reach for and grab their catch, and as an interest in more than fish develops between one couple. Momentarily finding herself alone with one man, a young woman initially feigns annoyance as her would-be partner flirts, moving away as he approaches, a broad smile stretching across his face (Plate 41). He picks a flower blossom and places it by her right ear, then playfully mimes splashing her with water. The woman raises her fishing tray to hide their faces as he leans in to pinch first one cheek, then the other. While the couple remains in place, hiding behind the fishing tray (which they move side-to-side with their hands, following the rhythm of the music), their fellow fisherfolk sneak back on stage, also covering their faces with their fishing trays and traps. Having surrounded the two sweethearts, they startle them with shouts of 'Haa!' In embarrassment tinged with delight, the discovered couple stands centre stage, heads slightly bent, as their friends parade by, congratulating and teasing the pair on their way off the stage. Left alone once more, they prepare to part, but, before doing so, the young man reminds his partner not to reveal their plans to meet again: he places his index finger before his lips to signal their secret pact. As they back away from each other, they wave goodbye, content with the knowledge that they will meet again.

Official performance programs in the 1990s have described this dance as one which highlights the abundance of one of the country's greatest natural resources—fish. It also highlights a traditional view of the encounter between young men and women. The

41. In this scene from the Fishing Dance, a
young man teases the woman he fancies by
picking up her fishing tray. Performed by
dancers of the University of Fine Arts, 1992.
(Toni Samantha Phim)

women, hard-working yet shy, turn their gaze away from the men
when the latter become too bold. Feigned rejection invites
increased attention, even aggression. With tight controls on social
encounter between the sexes, clandestine meetings are a particularly frequent leitmotiv of popular expression, and undoubtedly
play a principal role in social and sexual encounter particularly in the
countryside. None the less, young women are scorned if caught
meeting a man in secret. The activities of women are regulated or
limited to lessen the chance of scandal in the family. In the Fishing
Dance, the woman in the leading role responds cautiously to the
advances of the young man, as society expects she should. The

encounter is public before it becomes private. And even then, the privacy is only momentary. The scene of the short-lived tryst inevitably elicits giggles from the audience, both in reaction to the facial expressions of the performers and in response to this public portrayal of something often kept private.

In fact, for all the dance's traditionalist, rural cultural references, it employs unexpected gestural resources. Placing the index finger over the lips and waving goodbye are distinctly Western gestures that are out of place in a traditional Khmer context. The dance makes use of both the 'indigenous' and the 'foreign', the 'traditional' and the 'modern', in its depiction of the breaking of social rules by the young couple. Such transpositions were commonly projected through film and other mass media in Phnom Penh in the 1960s. This no doubt accounts for part of the humour of the scene, when the country lovers begin acting like Westerners or city-dwellers. The Fishing Dance provides a good example of how 'traditional indigenous' and 'modern foreign' elements may be mixed at will to form a certain reflection of a society animated at once by cultural continuity and change.

The choreography of folk dances created at the university is often based on the fundamental distinction between the sexes. Symmetry is a central motif, with men and women alternately separated according to sex and then paired off in couples. Encounter between the sexes may not always be as directly addressed as it is in the Fishing Dance, yet it is inevitably a structuring theme.

Though also charged with sexual meaning, a different sort of atmosphere is evoked in the Good Crops Dance, a piece inspired by visits to the mountainous northeast. Good Crops opens with six men in squatting position, beating handheld knobbed gongs. They rise, circle once around, and proceed off the stage, all the while stepping to the rhythm of the gongs. This is a reference to a particular manner of paying homage to the local ancestral spirits which the Royal University artists had observed among the Tumpuon minority.

Remaining on stage are six other men, all of whom had been standing immobile. Dressed in striped loincloths topped with long, red sashes wrapped about their waists, they sport red scarves around

their heads and wear bone earrings. They carry pairs of long wooden poles which they use to mimic the gestures of the upland rice planting system practiced by the Tumpuon and others. In this system, the fields are punctured with poles, not plowed. Rice seed is then strewn into the holes. The dancers strike the floor with the pole in one hand while simultaneously tapping the floor with the heel of the opposite foot. They step on the foot which has just tapped while preparing to shift to the other side. This is repeated as the women, dressed in black wraparound strapless dresses with horizontal stripes, sparkling silver headbands, long shimmering earrings, bone necklaces, and brass bangles, enter, set to follow the rhythm of the pounding by dropping rice seeds where the men have punctured the earth.

The dancers make their way off stage, only to reappear with additional accoutrements. The women wear baskets attached to belts around their waists; the men have baskets on their backs. Both women and men imitate the harvesting of the rice crop, reaching out to pull the unhusked rice from the stalks, and placing the kernels in the basket. The choreographic patterns change as they dance in lines and circles, upstage and downstage, sometimes holding their baskets before them (Plate 42). Men with gongs join them for a celebration of the harvest as the dance concludes.

Both the Good Crops and the Fishing dances, along with most theatrical folk dances, are performed to the accompaniment of *mohori* music. When on a concert stage, the ensemble is usually in the orchestra pit or hidden in the wings. In an outdoor setting, the musicians are generally set on stage with the dancers, but off to one side.

Theatrical folk dance melodies are traditional tunes whose lyrics have been reworked to fit the theme of the dance. As they have also been repeatedly reworked to fit the politics of the day, the lyrics are in themselves valuable historical documents, demonstrating at once the role of theatrical folk dance in nation building and changing perceptions of the nation.

A good example of this process is the history of the Pestle Dance. This was originally a popular folk dance, with repartee singing and lyrics describing the process of preparing harvested

42. Dancers of the University of Fine Arts depict
highlanders in the Good Crops Dance, 1990.
(Toni Samantha Phim)

rice: threshing, pounding, and so on. The Pestle Dance was revised
and refined by professional actors in Phnom Penh in the 1960s.
New lyrics were written:

Cambodia, at night
under the light of the full moon ...
Together Khmers harmoniously till the land
Following the five-year plan of the Prince ...

In the 1970s, once the royalty had gone into exile, the lyrics
were altered to eliminate references to the Prince. In addition, the
song now clearly set the dancers apart from the villagers they were

ostensibly portraying by beginning with 'Today, we student performers are happy, singing and dancing the Pestle Dance.'

Even the Khmer Rouge employed this melody, with costuming and gestures similar to other dances created during their regime: performers in black with checkered scarves marched to new lyrics extolling the revolution.

In the 1980s, after the ouster of the Khmer Rouge, and with a new government in place, the lyrics were again transformed. The words draw attention to recent history:

The youth of Cambodia
have moved beyond their suffering ...
Their main concern
is improving the economy ...

It is not surprising that the messages conveyed in theatrical folk dances are subject to modification according to changing world-views. Indeed the dances were created in a particular historical context, and though they were no doubt intended to serve primarily cultural ends, they stand as a good example of how inextricable the cultural and the political are. Choreography and melody have, however, for the most part remained unchanged. In fact, the resilience of the themes, codified movement, and music of theatrical folk dances through the stormy decades following their creation suggests that they quickly became a medium of expression that has responded to a very real and uninterrupted need as Cambodia struggles for existence in the modern world.

1. There also exists a royal *Trot* ceremony, which is characterized more by spirit possession than by dance, and is traditionally performed as a kind of annual exorcism of evil from the king or the palace, symbols of the nation.

2. Eveline Porée-Maspero, *Etude sur les Rites Agraires Cambodgiens*, Tome 1, Paris, Mouton, 1962, p. 220.

Glossary

Achar (អាចារ្យ). Male lay ritual specialist.

Angkor or *Angkorian Empire* (អង្គរ). Khmer empire which ruled over much of mainland South-East Asia from the ninth to the fifteenth century; name of region which was the seat of the Empire, in what is now Siem Reap Province.

Angkor Vat (អង្គរវត្ត). Twelfth-century temple located in Siem Reap Province.

Angkut (អង្គទ). Monkey warrior; ally of Hanuman in the *Reamker*.

Apsara (អប្សរ ឬ អប្សរា). Celestial woman; celestial dancer.

Ayong (អាយ៉ង). Shadow theatre featuring small articulated puppets; also called *sbaek touc*.

Chha banchos (ឆាបញ្ចុះ). Fixed series of fundamental dance postures and movements; also called *kbach baat*.

Chhayam (ឆៃយ៉ាំ). Comic, improvised dance accompanied by long drums which often precedes a ceremonial parade.

Hanuman (ហនុមាន). Rama's monkey general in the *Reamker*.

Indrajit (ឥន្ទ្រជិត). One of Ravana's warrior sons in the *Reamker*.

Kambu (កម្ពុ). A legendary founder of Cambodia.

Kampuchea (កម្ពុជា). Khmer name of Cambodia.

Kancha or *kanchae* (កញ្ញា ឬ កំញែ). Tall bamboo poles with rattling seeds attached, played as rhythmic accompaniment in some folk dances.

Kbach baat (ក្បាច់បាត). Fixed series of fundamental dance postures and movements; also called *chha banchos*.

Kben (កើ្បន). Traditional pantaloons fashioned by wrapping a length of cloth around the lower body, and twisting and pulling ends through the legs to fasten at the waist in the back.

Khmer (ខ្មែរ). Cambodian; majority ethnic group and language of Cambodia.

Kroma (ក្រមា). Traditional checkered scarf.

Kumbhakar (កុម្ភការ). One of Ravana's brothers in the *Reamker*.

Lakhon (ល្ខោន). Theatre; drama.

Lakhon khol (ល្ខោនខោល). All-male dance–drama.

Lakhon luong (ល្ខោនហ្លួង). 'King's drama'; classical or court dance.

Lakhon preah reach tröap (ល្ខោនព្រះរាជទ្រព្យ). 'Drama of royal heritage'; classical or court dance.

Lanka (លង្កា). Island kingdom of the ogre Reab in the *Reamker*.

Maha Eysei (មហាឫសី). Mythical sage and supreme guardian of the arts.

Mera (មេរ៉ា). A legendary progenitor of the Khmer people.

Moni Mekhala (មុនីមេខលា). Goddess of the seas; Ream Eyso's adversary in a classical dance-drama.

Nang sbaek (ណាំងស្បែក). Shadow theatre featuring large puppets; also called *sbaek thom*.

Neak ta (អ្នកតា). Local or ancestral spirit.

Neang Seda (នាងសីតា). Princess Sita in the *Reamker*.

Peur (ពឺរ). An ethnic minority group in Cambodia.

Phnom Penh (ភ្នំពេញ). Capital of Cambodia.

Pracheapriy (ប្រជាប្រិយ). Popular.

Preah Leak (ព្រះលក្ស្មណ៍). Prince Laksmana (Rama's brother) in the *Reamker*.

Preah Pisnukar (ព្រះពិស្ណុការ). Legendary architect of Angkor Vat and one patron of the arts.

Preah Ream (ព្រះរាម). Prince Rama in the *Reamker*.

Propeiney (ប្រពៃណី). Tradition; traditional; folk.

Punyakay (បុញ្ញកាយ). One of Ravana's nieces in the *Reamker*.

Rama. See Ream.

Ramayana. Indian epic tale known throughout Asia.

Ravana. See Reab.

Reab (រាពណ៍). Ravana, king of the ogres in the *Reamker*.

Ream Eyso (រាមស្ងួរ ឬ រាមឥសូរ). Ogre adversary of Moni Mekhala in a classical dance-drama.

Reamker (រាមកេរ្តិ៍). Khmer version of the *Ramayana*.

Roam vong (រាំវង់). A popular social dance in which a group of people moves counter-clockwise to a three or four beat rhythm in one large circle (*vong*).

Robam (របាំ). Dance.

Robam boran (របាំបុរាណ). 'Ancient dance'; classical or court dance.

Robam pracheapriy (របាំប្រជាប្រិយ). Theatrical or popular folk dance.

Robam propeiney (របាំប្រពៃណី). Ceremonial folk dance; can be used as a general term for all folk dance.

Sampeah (សំពះ). Gesture of prayer; respectful greeting: hands raised with palms placed together.

Sampeah kru (សំពះគ្រូ). Respectful greeting to a teacher; ceremony of salutation to deities, spirits, and teachers.

Sbaek thom (ស្បែកធំ). Shadow theatre featuring large puppets; also called *nang sbaek*.

Sbaek touc (ស្បែកតូច). Shadow theatre featuring small articulated puppets; also called *ayong*.

Seda. See Neang Seda.

Shiva (ព្រះសិវៈ ឬ ព្រះឥសូរ). A Brahmanic god.

Tang Tok (តាំងតុ). Cultural exhibition of crafts, produce, and arts from around the country, held under royal auspices.

Tevoda (ទេវតា). Deities.

Trot (ត្រុដិ). A kind of ceremonial folk dance.

Trot Neang Meov (ត្រុដិនាងម៉េវ). One version of the *Trot* ceremonial folk dance.

Tumpuon (ទំពួន). An ethnic minority group in Cambodia.

Vat Phnom (វត្តភ្នំ). Sacred site of Phnom Penh's foundation.

Vishnu (ព្រះវិស្ណុ ឬ ព្រះនារាយណ៍). Brahmanic god whose many earthly incarnations include Prince Rama.

Note: Musical instruments and ensembles are described in 'A Note on Music'.

Select Bibliography

Aymonier, Etienne, *Le Cambodge*, 3 volumes, Paris, Ernest Leroux, 1901–4.

Baradat, R., 'Les Samrês ou Peârs, population primitive de l'Ouest du Cambodge', *Bulletin de l'Ecole Française d'Extrême-Orient*, XLI, 1 (1941).

Brunet, Jacques, *Nang Sbek: Théâtre d'Ombres Dansé du Cambodge*, Berlin, Institut International d'Etudes Comparatives de la Musique, 1969.

Chap Pin, *Robam Pracheapriy Khmer* [Khmer Popular/Folk Dances], Phnom Penh, Buddhist Institute, 1964.

Cœdès, George, *Inscriptions du Cambodge*, 8 volumes, Hanoi and Paris, Ecole Française d'Extrême-Orient, 1937–66.

Cravath, Paul, 'Earth in Flower: An Historical and Descriptive Study of the Classical Dance Drama of Cambodia', Ph.D. thesis, University of Hawaii, 1985.

Groslier, Bernard-Philippe, *Inscriptions du Bayon, Mémoires Archéologiques 3*, Paris, Ecole Française d'Extrême-Orient, 1973.

Groslier, Georges, *Danseuses Cambodgiennes Anciennes et Modernes*, Paris, Augustin Challamel, 1913.

Jessup, Helen and Zéphir, Thierry (eds.), *Sculpture of Angkor and Ancient Cambodia*, New York, Thames and Hudson, 1997.

Leclère, Adhémar, *Cambodge: Fêtes civiles et religieuses*, Paris, Imprimerie Nationale, 1917.

Levy, Paul, 'Le Leng Trot ou Danses Rituelles et Rustiques du Nouvel An Khmer', *Seksa Khmer*, 3–4 (1981): 59–85; 5 (1982): 61–102; 6 (1983): 109–33; 7 (1984): 187–213.

Nut, Suppya Hélène, *Le théâtre royal khmer*, Cahiers d'Etudes Franco-Cambodgiennes, Centre Culturel et de Coopération Linguistique du Service Culturel de l'Ambassade de France, Phnom Penh, 1996.

Pich [Pech] Tum Kravel, *Sbek Thom: Khmer Shadow Theatre*, Phnom Penh, UNESCO and Southeast Asia Program, Cornell University, 1995.

Porée-Maspero, Eveline, *Etudes sur les Rites Agraires,* 3 volumes, Paris, Mouton, 1962–9.

Pou, Saveros, *Etudes sur le Rāmakerti (XVIè-XVIIè siècles)*, Paris, Ecole Française d'Extrême-Orient, 1977.

————, *Rāmakerti (XVIè-XVIIè siècles)*, translated and with commentary by, Paris, Ecole Française d'Extrême-Orient, 1977.

————, *Rāmakerti (XVIè-XVIIè siècles): Texte khmer publié*, Paris, Ecole Française d'Extrême-Orient, 1979.

————, *Rāmakerti II (Deuxième version du Rāmāyaṇa khmer): Texte khmer, traduction et annotations*, Paris, Ecole Française d'Extrême-Orient, 1982.

Pou, Saveros and Guiriati, Giovanni, *Etude de Musicologie*, Cahiers d'Etudes Franco-Cambodgiennes, Centre Culturel et de Coopération Linguistique du Service Culturel de L'Ambassade de France, Phnom Penh, 1995.

Sam, Chan Moly and Sam, Sam-Ang, *Khmer Folk Dance*, Newington, Connecticut, Khmer Studies Institute, 1987.

Sam, Sam-Ang, 'The Pin Peat Ensemble: Its History, Music, and Context', Ph.D. thesis, Wesleyan University, 1988.

Sem Sara, 'Lakhon Khol at the Village of Vat-Svay-Andet', *New Cambodge*, 21 (November), 1972, pp. 46–57.

Shapiro, Toni, 'Dance and the Spirit of Cambodia', Ph.D. thesis, Cornell University, 1994.

Tauch Chhuong, *Battambang Samay Lok Mchas* [Battambang in the Era of Lord Governor], Battambang, Association of Researchers, 1974; 2nd edition Phnom Penh, Cedoreck, 1994.

Thompson, Ashley, 'Mémoires du Cambodge', Ph.D. thesis, Université de Paris 8, 1999.

Université Royale des Beaux-Arts, *Musique Khmère*, Phnom Penh, 1969.

————, *Rāmker (Rāmāyaṇa khmer)*, Phnom Penh, Imprimerie Sangkum Reastr Niyum, 1969.

Index

References in brackets refer to Plate numbers; those in brackets and italics to Colour Plate numbers.

CHINA

BURMA
(MYANMAR)

THAILAND LAOS VIETNAM

Angkor

CAMBODIA

M A L A Y S I A

SINGAPORE

Borneo

Sumatra

I N D O N

Java

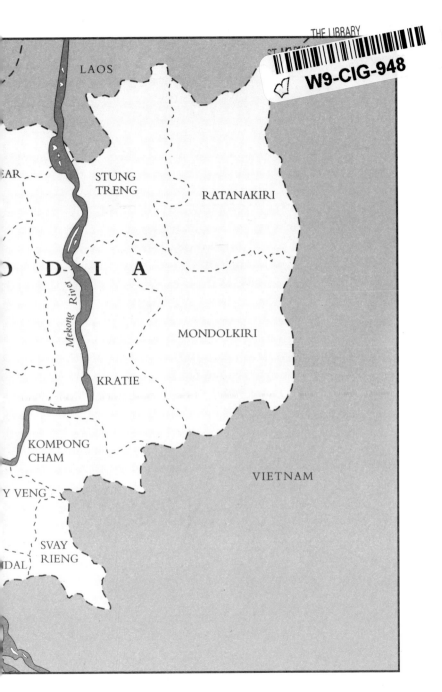

LAOS

EAR

STUNG
TRENG

RATANAKIRI

O   D   I   A

Mekong River

MONDOLKIRI

KRATIE

KOMPONG
CHAM

VIETNAM

Y VENG

SVAY
RIENG

DAL